NORTH AMERICAN GAME ANIMALS

THE HUNTING & FISHING LIBRARY®

By David R. Maas

DAVID MAAS is an all-around outdoorsman with a passion for bowhunting trophy whitetails and searching for their shed antlers. He worked as a fishing guide in Alaska and is currently a Book Development Leader for The Hunting & Fishing Library®.

COWLES
Creative Publishing

President: Iain Macfarlane

NORTH AMERICAN GAME ANIMALS

Author and Book Development Leader: David R. Maas
Executive Editor, Outdoors Group: Don Oster
Hunting & Fishing Library Director and Editor: Dick Sternberg
Contributing Writer: Mike Hehner
Project Manager: Denise Bornhausen
Senior Art Director: Dave Schelitzche
Art Director: Kathlynn Henthorne
Researcher: Jim Moynagh
V. P. Development Planning and Production: Jim Bindas
Senior Publishing Production Manager: Laurie Gilbert
Copy Editor: Janice Cauley
Senior Desktop Publishing Specialists: Joe Fahey, Laurie Kristensen
Production Staff: Mike Schauer
Illustrator: Thomas Boll
Cover Photo: Steve Maas

Contributing Photographers: Erwin and Peggy Bauer, Craig Blacklock, Boone and Crockett Club, Denver Bryan, Robert Campbell, Daniel J. Cox, Dembinsky & Associates, Jeanne Drake, Michael Francis, The Green Agency, Mike Hehner, Lee Kline, Gary Kramer, Lon E. Lauber, Tom and Pat Leeson, Steve Maas, Bill Marchel, Minden Pictures, Don Oster, Photo Researchers Inc., Publiphoto, Lynn Rogers, David Sams, Ron Spomer, Tom Stack & Associates

Cooperating Individuals and Agencies: Nancy Anderson, National Biological Service; Judith Hudson Beattie, Hudson's Bay Company; Marcy Bishop, U.S. Fish and Wildlife Service; Sam Blankenship, California Department of Fish and Game; Breck Carmichael, South Carolina Department of Natural Resources; Anne Gunn, Department of Renewable Resources; Cathy Harms and Ken Whitten, Alaska Department of Fish and Game; Fred Harrington, Mount St. Vincent University; Nicholas R. Holler, Alabama Cooperative Fish and Wildlife Research Unit; Doug Humphreys, Texas Parks and Wildlife Department; John Litvaitis, University of New Hampshire; Al Miller, South Dakota Department of Game, Fish and Parks; Susan Reneau and Chris Tonkinson, Boone and Crockett Club; Dave Roberts, U.S. Department of Interior; Rocky Mountain Elk Foundation; Sean Sharpe, British Columbia Wildlife Branch; Phil Smith, Arizona Game and Fish Department; Leah Soper, Newfoundland Department of Natural Resources; San Stiver, Nevada Department of Wildlife; Tom Thornton, Oregon Department of Fish and Wildlife; Steve Torres, California Department of Fish and Game; Raul Valdez, New Mexico State University; Mark Zornes, Wyoming Game and Fish Department

Printed on American paper by: R. R. Donnelley & Sons Co.
00 99 98 97 / 5 4 3 2 1

Library of Congress
Cataloging-in-Publication Data

Maas, David R.
North American game animals / by David R. Maas
p. cm. – (The Hunting & fishing library)
Includes index.
ISBN 0-86573-048-2 (hc)
1. Game and game birds–North America. 2. Mammals–North America.
3. Hunting–North America. I Title. II. Series.
SK40.M25 1995
799.2'6'097–dc20   95-18908

Books available from the publisher: *The Art of Freshwater Fishing, Cleaning & Cooking Fish, Fishing With Live Bait, Largemouth Bass, Panfish, The Art of Hunting, Fishing With Artificial Lures, Walleye, Smallmouth Bass, Dressing & Cooking Wild Game, Freshwater Gamefish of North America, Trout, Secrets of the Fishing Pros, Fishing Rivers & Streams, Fishing Tips & Tricks, Fishing Natural Lakes, White-tailed Deer, Northern Pike & Muskie, America's Favorite Fish Recipes, Fishing Man-made Lakes, The Art of Fly Tying, America's Favorite Wild Game Recipes, Advanced Bass Fishing, Upland Game Birds, North American Game Animals, North American Game Birds, Advanced Whitetail Hunting, Understanding Whitetails, Fly-Fishing Equipment & Skills, Fly Fishing for Trout in Streams–Subsurface Techniques, Fly-Tying Techniques & Patterns, Fly Rod Gamefish–The Freshwater Species, Bowhunting Equipment & Skills, Wild Turkey, Muzzleloading, Duck Hunting, Venison Cookery, Game Bird Cookery*

Contents

Introduction

This book is a complete reference guide to the game animals of North America. Although it is aimed primarily at hunters, every wildlife enthusiast will be engrossed by its wealth of fascinating information and extraordinary color photos of animals in their natural habitat.

The book details the basic biology of every North American mammal pursued by hunters, from Alaskan brown bears to Abert's squirrels. It does not cover upland birds and waterfowl, which will be the subject of a soon-to-be-published companion volume, *North American Game Birds*.

You'll learn how to identify the animals, where to find them throughout the year, how fast they grow, how long they live, what they eat, how they detect danger and how they breed and interact with other members of the species.

Many North American game animals have a number of varieties, or subspecies, that differ slightly in size, coloration or range. The book covers each subspecies of significance to hunters and shows you the important differences. It also shows you how to differentiate between the sexes.

Besides biological facts, the book provides information for hunters not found in ordinary animal identification books. You'll learn the basic techniques for hunting each animal, along with tips on recognizing tracks, droppings and other important sign. We even describe the table quality of the meat.

Most big-game hunters dream of taking a trophy animal, so we've included information on world-record antlers, horns and skulls, as compiled by the Boone and Crockett Club, the official keeper of big-game records. You'll be astounded by rarely seen photos of the most spectacular racks ever taken.

After paging through *North American Game Animals* and coming face-to-face with a snarling grizzly bear, watching bighorn rams clashing horns or seeing a red fox pouncing on a mouse, you'll realize that the book contains the most sensational collection of animal photographs ever assembled. The shots were taken by some of the country's premier wildlife photographers, including Denver Bryan, Jeanne Drake, Michael Francis and dozens of others.

Game biologists from around the country contributed to the text, assuring accurate, up-to-date information and eliminating the animal-behavior myths that permeate so many other wildlife books.

The key element separating the expert hunter from the novice is a thorough understanding of the quarry's behavior. Not only is this book an indispensable reference source, it lays the groundwork for hunting success.

Hoofed Animals

Order Artiodactyla

The name *Artiodactyla*, meaning "even-toed," refers to the fact that these animals have four toes per foot. The two main toes make up the hoof and the two

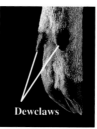

Dewclaws

smaller ones form the *dewclaws* (left), which are higher on the leg and do not normally touch the ground.

Most hoofed animals have a four-chambered stomach. They quickly swallow their food and store it in the largest chamber, called the *rumen*. The food then passes to the second chamber, where it is formed into pellets, called the *cud*. As the

animal rests in cover, it regurgitates the food and *chews its cud*, or *ruminates*. The food then passes through two more chambers and is finally digested. The rumination process reduces the amount of time an animal must spend in feeding areas, where they are usually exposed to predators.

With the exception of wild boar and peccary, hoofed animals have antlers or horns, which may grow to magnificent size – an important aspect of the hunt for many big-game enthusiasts.

Antlers, grown annually, emerge in spring as a bony projection covered with a fuzzy membrane, or *velvet*, that provides nourishment. The fully developed antlers lose their velvet in fall and are shed in winter. Females of antlered species, except caribou, rarely grow antlers.

Horns grow continuously through life and are never shed. They consist of a sheath of *keratin*, a protein found in hair and nails, growing over a bony projection from the skull. Both sexes have horns, but those of the male are larger.

White-Tailed Deer
(Odocoileus virginianus)

Common Names – Whitetail, Virginia deer.

Description – The white-tailed deer is North America's most popular big-game animal. Its ability to thrive in a variety of habitats explains why more than 20 million whitetails now inhabit the U.S. and Canada.

■ **Coues'**
□ **Other Whitetails**

Whitetails are reddish brown in spring and summer; brownish gray in fall and winter. The hair on the throat, muzzle, belly, inside of the legs and underside of the tail is white. Northern and eastern deer are darker than western and southern deer.

Fawns have a reddish coat covered with white spots for camouflage. They shed this coat in fall and grow a thick, brown winter coat with no spots.

Doe and fawn in summer coats

Bucks have antlers with points that normally grow upward from an unforked main beam. A doe rarely has antlers. Most bucks have *typical* racks, meaning the antlers are fairly symmetrical, with approximately the same number of points on each main beam. *Nontypical* racks are not symmetrical, and the points may grow in any direction from the main beam.

Important Subspecies – Up to 30 subspecies have been identified, each varying slightly in size, color and geographic range. Northern subspecies, such as the Dakota *(Odocoileus virginianus dakotensis)* and northern woodland whitetail *(Odocoileus virginianus borealis)*, are the largest; Key deer *(Odocoileus virginianus clavium)*, the smallest. These tiny residents of the Florida Keys are classified as endangered species. Coues' deer *(Odocoileus virginianus couesi)* are the smallest huntable whitetail. Their antlers, ears and tail are larger in proportion to their body than those of other whitetails. They live in the mountains of Arizona, New Mexico and Mexico.

Whitetail buck in fall coat

The Boone and Crockett Club keeps separate records for Coues' deer; all other varieties are classified simply as "Whitetail Deer."

Age and Growth – At birth, fawns average 5 pounds. By age 4 or 5, most animals have reached full size, in terms of body weight and antler development. Mature northern bucks usually weigh from 175 to 250 pounds and measure 5 to 6 feet from nose to tail. Exceptional northern bucks may reach 8 feet in length and weigh more than 350 pounds. Coues' bucks weigh 100 to 150 pounds and measure 4 to 5 feet in length. A doe normally weighs about 25 percent less than a buck.

A doe may live as long as 22 years; a buck, 10 years. In heavily hunted areas, however, bucks seldom live past the age of 3.

Senses – Sense of smell and night vision, excellent; hearing and daytime vision, very good.

A large portion of a whitetail's brain is used to identify and interpret odors. This explains why successful hunters pay such close attention to wind direction and do whatever else is necessary to prevent deer from detecting their scent.

Whitetails are noted for their ability to detect even the slightest motion, even when the light is so dim that a human could barely see. Their large, cupped ears make good sound collectors and are spaced widely enough to enable the animal to pinpoint sounds by triangulation.

Bucks that survive through three hunting seasons have mastered the use of their senses so well that it is unlikely they will ever be taken by a hunter.

Coues' buck

Sign – Tracks of adult deer measure about 3 inches long (p. 119). Distinct trails can be found between bedding and feeding areas. The droppings, deposited in clusters, are ½ to 1 inch long and slightly elongated. The oval-shaped beds measure 2½ to 4 feet long. Daytime beds are in dense cover; nightime beds, in open, grassy fields.

In fall, bucks make *rubs* (below) and *scrapes* (right) as part of their breeding ritual.

Social Interaction – Family groups, consisting of a doe, her fawns and sometimes her yearlings, spend most of the year together. Bucks are usually solitary, but may form small bands in summer. The largest bucks are loners year-round.

In a severe winter, dozens of whitetails may gather in *deer yards,* protected areas where they can easily find food. Deer yards may draw family groups from up to 10 miles away.

Whitetails communicate with visual signals and vocalizations. Casual tail wagging means all is well. But stamping the front feet or holding the tail horizontally is an alarm signal. Bounding off with tail held high, or *flagging* (right), means danger is imminent.

Flagging whitetail

Deer snort when they're alarmed or can't identify a strange object or smell. Soon after snorting, they usually take flight. A fawn makes a high-pitched bawl when separated from the doe, and other deer may bawl when injured. Bucks commonly grunt when searching for a mate or tending a doe in heat.

Breeding – Most whitetails breed from late October to early January; Coues' deer, in February or March. Prior to the breeding period, or *rut*, bucks rake small trees and bushes with their antlers, removing the bark. These rubs serve to announce their presence to other deer.

Whitetail rubs

Whitetail scrape

During the rut, a buck signals his desire to breed by pawing out oblong depressions in the ground and scenting them with urine. These scrapes, which measure 1 to 4 feet long, are usually made beneath an overhanging branch, which he licks and rubs with his head to leave additional scent.

The rut begins when the first does come into heat, or *estrus*. A buck pursuing a doe moves more during the day than he normally would, explaining why hunting during the rut is so popular.

In the North, the rut peaks in early November; in the South, mid- to late November. A buck generally stays with a doe 1 or 2 days, often breeding her several times. When she no longer accepts him, he leaves her to find another doe. Any doe that is not bred by the end of the rut comes into heat again a month later.

Similar-size bucks may battle to determine breeding rights. With heads lowered, they lunge at each other and smash antlers, each pushing and twisting to knock the other to the ground. Occasionally, their antlers become locked, and the animals starve or are taken by predators.

In spring, a pregnant doe goes off by herself to give birth. A first-time breeder usually delivers a single fawn; an older doe, twins or, more rarely, triplets.

Habitat – Found in forests, agricultural lands, mountain foothills, plains, river bottoms and brushlands, whitetails can adapt to most any habitat with adequate food, cover and water. In fact, some of the biggest bucks live in the wooded suburbs of large cities.

Coues' deer inhabit steep mountains, usually at elevations of 4,000 to 8,000 feet. They prefer oak, juniper and pinyon pine forests with deep, wide canyons and streams bordered by heavy brush.

Food Habits – During the hunting season, whitetails usually feed after dark. Around sunset, does and their young leave bedding thickets and meander toward feeding areas. Small- to medium-size bucks

World-record typical whitetail

World-record non-typical whitetail

move a little later and large bucks move last. Deer feed for a few hours and then bed nearby to rest and chew their cud. They feed again during the last few hours of darkness. Big bucks usually return to their daytime bedding sanctuaries well before sunrise; lesser bucks and doe groups, at daybreak.

In fall and winter, deer browse on small twigs and branches of trees and shrubs, such as willow, maple, mountain mahogany, dogwood and white cedar. They also eat clover, acorns, corn, alfalfa, wheat, oats and soybeans. In spring and summer, they graze on grasses and other green plants.

Movement – A whitetail spends most of its life in a small area that provides adequate food, cover and water. A doe normally stays within 1 square mile; a buck, 2. Deer living in vast forests or open plains roam more widely.

Whitetails normally move about by walking or trotting. When spooked, however, they bound away with graceful leaps or gallop at speeds up to 40 mph. Good swimmers, they commonly cross big rivers or lakes several miles wide.

Population – During the twentieth century, the North American whitetail population grew from less than a million to more than 20 million, mainly because of the increase in edge habitat created by farming and other land development. In many areas where whitetails are not hunted, such as suburbs of metropolitan areas, they have overpopulated their range.

Hunting Strategies – One of the most popular techniques is stand-hunting. By placing a tree stand along a recently used trail between a bedding and feeding area, you can easily surprise moving deer. Still-hunting involves moving a short distance, stopping with your back against a tree, and watching for 15 minutes to an hour to spot a moving deer before it spots you. Driving thick patches of cover, such as wood lots or river corridors, flushes bedded deer to posters.

The glass-and-stalk method accounts for most Coues' deer. Hunters climb to a high elevation in early morning to spot the deer they want, and then stalk to within shooting range.

Trophy Records – Following are the Boone and Crockett records for each whitetail category:

•Typical – $213^{5/8}$ points, with an inside spread of $27^{2/8}$ inches; shot in Biggar, Saskatchewan, in 1993.

•Non-typical – $333^{7/8}$ points, with a spread of $23^{3/8}$ inches; found in St. Louis County, Missouri, in 1981.

•Coues' typical – 143 points, with a spread of $15^{3/8}$ inches; shot in Pima County, Arizona, in 1953.

•Coues' non-typical – $158^{4/8}$ points, with a spread of $12^{6/8}$ inches; found in Santa Cruz County, Arizona, in 1988.

Eating Quality – Excellent; the meat is tender and mild, especially if the animals were feeding on acorns or agricultural crops. Browse-fed deer may have a stronger taste.

Rocky Mountain and desert (inset) mule deer bucks

Mule & Black-Tailed Deer
(Odocoileus hemionus)

Important Subspecies – Seven subspecies of *Odocoileus hemionus* are recognized, including five varieties of mule deer, or "mulies," and two kinds of blacktails.

The subspecies most important to hunters are:

• Rocky Mountain mule deer *(Odocoileus hemionus hemionus)*, the most numerous of the seven, found throughout most of the western U.S. and Canada.

• Desert mule deer *(Odocoileus hemionus crooki)*, found in Arizona, New Mexico, Texas and northern Mexico.

• Columbia black-tailed deer *(Odocoileus hemionus columbianus)*, found along the Pacific coast from northern British Columbia to central California.

• Sitka black-tailed deer *(Odocoileus hemionus sitkensis)*, found from southeast Alaska to northern British Columbia, including the Queen Charlotte Islands.

Description – Unlike whitetails, mulies and blacktails have antlers with a forked main beam. Rocky Mountain mule deer have the widest and tallest racks, followed by desert mulies, Columbia blacktails and Sitka blacktails.

Blacktails get their name from their dark brown to black tail; mulies, from their foot-long, mule-like ears. The ears of blacktails are noticeably shorter, usually 6 or 7 inches long.

A muley's coat is reddish brown in summer; grayish brown in fall and

MULE DEER

• Distinct white rump patch; upper two-thirds of the tube-shaped tail is white, lower one-third, black (right)
• Adults have ears up to 1 foot in length
• Racks grow wider and taller than those of blacktails
• Bucks usually weigh 200 pounds or less
• Prefer fairly dry, open terrain

winter. The face, throat and belly are white. Rocky Mountain and desert mule deer, the largest subspecies, are distinguishable only by antler size.

Blacktails have an overall darker coloration than mulies, and more of the tail is dark (below).

Age and Growth – At birth, fawns weigh 5 to 8 pounds. They reach full size in about 3 years and may live up to 15. Rocky mountain and desert mule deer bucks measure 5 to 6 feet long and weigh 140 to 200 pounds, with an occasional trophy exceeding 400 pounds. A doe normally weighs 100 to 160 pounds. Columbia and Sitka blacktails are considerably smaller, weighing only about two-thirds as much.

Senses – Sense of smell, hearing and night vision, excellent; eyesight, very good. The animals constantly swivel their huge ears to pinpoint the location of any unusual noise, but they normally wait until they see or smell a threat before taking flight. They are quick to spot motion, even at long distances.

Sign – Tracks (p. 119) are similar in shape and size to those of a whitetail. Individual droppings measure ¾ to 1 inch long and are usually found in clusters.

During the rut, bucks rub their antlers on saplings, brush or fence poles. The rubbing serves as sparring practice for upcoming breeding battles and the bared wood signals a certain buck's claim to that territory. Unlike whitetail bucks, muley and blacktail bucks do not make scrapes.

Social Interaction – Most mulies and blacktails live in sexually segregated bands from late spring until fall, but the largest bucks are loners. As the breeding season begins, the bands start to mix. In winter, several bands may combine to form a herd that numbers several dozen.

Columbia blacktail buck

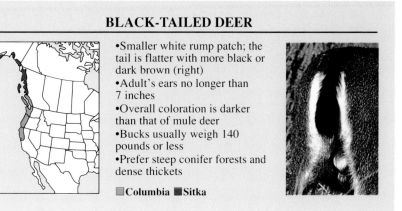

Sitka blacktail buck

BLACK-TAILED DEER

•Smaller white rump patch; the tail is flatter with more black or dark brown (right)
•Adult's ears no longer than 7 inches
•Overall coloration is darker than that of mule deer
•Bucks usually weigh 140 pounds or less
•Prefer steep conifer forests and dense thickets

■ Columbia ■ Sitka

Doe with fawns

Buck bachelor group

A dominant doe, or *matriarch,* leads each herd. The bucks, now without antlers, act passively toward each other and other herd members.

In spring, bucks separate from the herd and form "bachelor groups" (above). Fawns remain with the doe until she is ready to give birth the following spring. Afterward, she may allow them to rejoin the family unit.

Mulies and blacktails communicate in much the same manner as whitetails. Fawns make a whiney bawl when separated from the doe, and she responds with a high-pitched blat. Bucks grunt when searching for a doe in heat. Both sexes alert other deer to danger by snorting, stamping their front feet or flaring the hair on their rump patch.

Breeding – Mule deer breed from October to January, with the peak over most of their range in November or December. Blacktails breed from September to November.

The breeding habits of mule deer and blacktails are nearly identical to those of whitetails, but the bucks do not make scrapes.

In forested areas where mule deer and whitetail ranges overlap, the two may hybridize. Recent studies have shown that hybrids are easy targets for predators, because they lack the specialized survival instincts of the parents.

Habitat – Mule deer prefer drier, more open terrain than blacktails or whitetails. They thrive in a variety of habitats, including deserts, rolling prairies, desolate brushlands and mountains and foothills with sparse tree growth. Blacktails reside in steep coniferous forests and dense chaparral thickets along the Pacific coast.

Food Habits – Mulies and blacktails feed heavily in early morning and late afternoon. When hunting pressure is heavy, they may feed at night. In midday,

they bed down on high ridges or rocky terraces to rest and chew their cud. A muley's bedding site may be one or two miles from its feeding area, but a blacktail beds much closer, usually in the thickest cover available.

Mule deer rely heavily on willow leaves, fescue grass, bluegrass, alpine fireweed and wheat grass in summer. They browse on bitterbrush, Russian thistle, mountain mahogany and sagebrush in fall and winter. Blacktails feed mainly on bromegrass, filaree oak, manzanita and buckthorn. When the opportunity arises, both will eat acorns, berries, wildflowers, fungi and agricultural crops.

Movement – Deep snow high in the mountains forces mulies and blacktails to lower elevations, where the ground is snow-free. Mulies migrate as far as 50 miles, usually to foothills or prairies swept clean of snow by the wind. Those living in desert habitat often winter on sagebrush flats, using the sage for winter food.

Mulies and blacktails are known for their stiff-legged gait, called *stotting.* They move in pogo-stick fashion, with all four feet touching the ground simultaneously on each bound. Unlike a galloping whitetail, a stotting muley or blacktail can instantly change direction to cross uneven ground and ascend nearly vertical terrain. They can clear 8-foot obstacles with ease, and have been clocked at speeds of 35 mph.

Stotting mule deer

Population – At present, blacktail populations are stable, but mule deer appear to be undergoing a very

World-record typical Sitka blacktail

World-record typical mule deer

slow, almost imperceptible decline. Ongoing research indicates that overharvest of large mule deer bucks has resulted in more whitetail bucks breeding with doe mule deer. The population decline is caused by the hybrids' higher susceptibility to predators. It may take centuries to realize the full impact of this trend.

Hunting Strategies – Most mulies are taken using the glass-and-stalk technique. After climbing to the highest part of your hunting area long before sunrise, use binoculars or a spotting scope at first light to watch for feeding mule deer. If they're out of shooting range, plan a stalk that will get you close enough for a shot. Use ravines, boulders or brush to conceal your approach. Ideally, you should approach from above because a deer usually looks for danger from below.

You can intercept mulies moving between feeding and bedding areas by stand-hunting. Conceal yourself on a saddle between two ridges or in any other natural funnel.

When hunting pressure forces mule deer into heavier cover, try still-hunting the edges of steep ravines or driving brushy stream corridors to push the deer toward posters. Mulies have a unique habit that often works to the hunter's advantage: as the animals flee, they frequently stop at the crest of a hill and look back, offering one last shot.

Columbia blacktails are commonly taken in early season by stand-hunting. Place your stand downwind of a feeding area, such as a clear-cut or burn. Later, when the leaves are falling, try still-hunting along

mountain slopes and ridge tops. When you suspect blacktails are bedded down in isolated thickets, walk through the cover to drive them toward posters.

One of the best ways to locate Sitka blacktails is to run the shoreline of coastal islands or tidal rivers with a boat, checking the beaches and forest edges. When you spot a deer you want, pull the boat ashore and begin your stalk. Another effective method is still-hunting steep, rocky cliffs and open slopes. Trailing the animals after a fresh snow has also accounted for many trophies.

Trophy Records – For record-keeping purposes, all mule deer subspecies are considered simply "mule deer." Following are records for the mule deer and blacktail categories recognized by the Boone and Crockett Club:

•Mule deer typical – 226$\frac{4}{8}$ points, with an inside spread of 30$\frac{7}{8}$ inches; shot in Dolores County, Colorado, in 1972.

•Mule deer non-typical – 355$\frac{2}{8}$ points, with a spread of 22$\frac{1}{8}$ inches; taken in Chip Lake, Alberta, in 1926.

•Columbia blacktail typical – 182$\frac{2}{8}$ points, with a spread of 20$\frac{2}{8}$ inches; shot in Lewis County, Washington, in 1953.

•Sitka blacktail typical – 128 points, with a spread of 19$\frac{4}{8}$ inches; taken on Kodiak Island, Alaska, in 1985.

Eating Quality – Good to very good. Crop-fed deer have the best-tasting meat; sagebrush fed, the strongest. The meat is drier than beef.

Elk
(Cervus elaphus)

Roosevelt bull elk

Common Name – Wapiti.

Description – Among the largest hoofed animals in North America, elk have tan coats with long, dark-brown hair on the head and neck. The legs and belly are nearly black; the rump patch and tail, yellowish white.

Rocky Mountain
Roosevelt

Bulls may have antlers more than 5 feet long. Those with 6 points on each antler are called *royal* elk; 7 points, *imperial* elk; and 8 points, *monarchs*. Cow elk do not have antlers.

Important Subspecies – The Rocky Mountain, or American, elk is the most numerous subspecies, inhabiting much of the western U.S. and Canada. The Roosevelt, or Olympic, elk lives only in coastal areas of the Pacific Northwest and on Kodiak Island, Alaska. The two are nearly identical, but Rocky Mountain elk are smaller, with longer antlers that have a greater spread.

Two other subspecies, the Tule and Manitoban elk, exist in small numbers and are currently protected. Tule elk have a very limited range in California, and Manitoban elk are found primarily in provincial parks in Manitoba, Alberta, Saskatchewan and the Yukon.

The Merriam and eastern elk became extinct by the late 1700s, mainly from market hunting and clearing of land for agricultural purposes.

Age and Growth – At birth, calves weigh 20 to 45 pounds. Elk reach adult size by age 4 and live up to 15 years. Mature Roosevelt bulls weigh 700 to 1,100 pounds and measure 7 to 8½ feet long. Rocky Mountain bulls are slightly shorter and weigh 550 to 800 pounds. Cows weigh about 25 percent less than bulls.

Rocky Mountain bull elk

Senses – Sense of smell and hearing, excellent; eyesight, good. Elk usually detect hunters and wolves by smell. They quickly spot motion but often overlook a hunter sitting still.

Sign – Tracks (p. 119) measure about 4 inches long. Droppings take the form of pellets when elk are browsing; small, soft piles, when they are grazing. Wallows (right) are made by bulls using their antlers to scrape out large depressions in soft ground. As part of the breeding ritual, a bull urinates on

Typical elk wallow

the exposed earth and rolls around in it, covering himself with mud. Rubs, made while practice-fighting, announce a bull's presence to other elk. They resemble the rubs made by whitetails, but may be on larger trees.

Social Interaction – Cows, calves and young bulls live together year-round for protection from predators. Mature bulls commonly form small bands in summer and fall, or they may live alone until the mating season.

Elk harem

These bands have a social hierarchy, with lesser bulls challenging the dominant bull to sparring matches. The bands break up when the bulls shed their antlers, because they can no longer establish dominance.

During the breeding season, bulls *bugle* to call females and challenge other bulls in the area. The sound begins with a low-pitched bellow and progresses to a shrill, high-pitched whistle. Hunters use a variety of calls to mimic this sound and lure a bull into shooting range.

Calves make a high-pitched bleat when they're in danger. Cows emit a coughlike bark that tells the calves to seek cover; a nasal whine is an all-clear signal.

Breeding – Elk mate in September or October. The dominant bull, or *herd bull*, defends his harem of up to 30 cows (above) against the advances of younger bulls or other herd bulls. In these antler battles (below, left), which are much more violent than sparring matches, a bull must throw the challenger to the ground and chase him off to maintain his dominant rank.

If a cow is not bred the first time she comes into heat, she can still be bred during one of the next three cycles, which are 21 days apart. A cow normally gives birth to 1 calf (below, right); twins are rare.

Habitat – Found in mountainous regions with open meadows amid large stands of conifers. This edge habitat provides elk with food, security from predators and shelter from severe weather.

Bull elk in antler battle

Cow with calf

World-record typical
Rocky Mountain elk

Food Habits – Elk feed heavily from first light until late morning, and then bed nearby to rest and chew their cud. They feed again in late afternoon before bedding on steep mountain slopes around sunset. When hunting pressure is heavy, they commonly feed after dark.

In summer, elk graze on grasses, such as blue grass, brome, June grass and wheat grass, and on forbs, such as ragweed, clover and dandelion. In winter, they browse on willow, balsam, aspen, poplar and red osier dogwood.

Movement – Elk migrate up to 100 miles between summer and winter ranges, using the same routes each year. In late fall, deep snow in the high country makes feeding difficult, forcing cows and young bulls down to south-facing slopes with little snow. Adult bulls remain at higher elevations unless the snow becomes so deep they cannot move about. Then, they also move lower, but they don't go down as far as the rest of the herd.

In early spring, elk head back up the mountain, working their way toward north-facing, sun-shaded slopes where they can stay cool and find a good supply of grasses and forbs.

Migrating elk can trot great distances at 10 to 20 mph. They can sprint up to 35 mph when disturbed.

Population – Stable; a century ago, elk were found throughout much of North America, but a good share of their habitat was lost to land development.

Hunting Strategies – The most successful elk hunters ride horses into the high country, where they set up a base camp. This way, they can comfortably spend a week or more in the remote mountainous terrain where trophy bulls are normally found.

After finding sign that indicates elk are feeding or wallowing in a certain area, get above it and try stand-hunting from a ground blind or rocky outcrop. In midday, the best method is still-hunting wooded ridges to surprise elk bedded in heavy cover.

Many hunters consider calling the most exciting and effective technique for taking a trophy bull. Beginning at sunrise, blow an elk call to mimic the bugle of a young bull. The object is to draw in a herd bull eager to defend his harem against the intruder.

Trophy Records – Following are the Boone and Crockett records for each of the recognized elk categories:

•Rocky Mountain elk, typical – $442\frac{3}{8}$ points, with an inside spread of $45\frac{4}{8}$ inches; shot in Dark Canyon, Colorado, in 1899.

•Rocky Mountain elk, non-typical – $447\frac{1}{8}$ points, with a spread of $39\frac{7}{8}$ inches; taken in Gilbert Plains, Manitoba, in 1961.

•Roosevelt elk, typical – $388\frac{3}{8}$ points, with a spread of $36\frac{1}{8}$ inches; shot in Tsitika River, British Columbia, in 1989.

Eating Quality – Excellent; slightly darker than beef but similar in taste and texture.

Moose
(Alces alces)

Important Subspecies – Four have been identified. There are two types of Canada moose: the eastern Canada moose, *Alces alces americana*, found mainly in eastern

Canada and Maine; and the northwestern Canada moose, *Alces alces andersoni*, found in western Canada and Minnesota. Other types include: the Alaska-Yukon moose, *Alces alces gigas*, found in Alaska, the Yukon and the Northwest Territories; and the Wyoming or Shiras moose, *Alces alces shirasi*, from the Rocky Mountain region south of the Canada border west to the Pacific coast.

Description – The moose is North America's largest antlered animal. A bull may stand 7 feet tall at the shoulder and measure 10 feet long. They have large, palmated antlers with numerous points. Cows do not grow antlers. Moose have long legs, humped shoulders, a long head and a *dewlap* or *bell* hanging from the throat. Shiras and Canada moose have dark brown coats, grayish lower legs and brown undersides. Only minor differences in cranial measurements separate the two types of Canada moose. Alaska-Yukon moose are darker than the others, with many being completely black.

Age and Growth – Moose weigh 25 to 35 pounds at birth, grow to adult size in 4 to 5 years and live up to 18. Shiras bulls weigh 900 to 1,200 pounds; Canada bulls, 1,000 to 1,400 and Alaska-Yukon bulls, 1,400 to 1,800. Cows weigh about 25 percent less than bulls.

Senses – Sense of smell, excellent; hearing, good; eyesight, fair. Moose rely on their sense of smell to detect hunters and wolves, their only predators. They usually overlook a motionless hunter.

Sign – Tracks (p. 119) measure about 6 inches long. The prints cut deeply into soft ground, accounting for many of the portage trails connecting remote, northern lakes. The cylindrical droppings are 1 to

Alaska-Yukon bull moose shedding velvet

1¾ inches long. During the rut, bull moose thrash and break off saplings and brush with their antlers to display dominance. They use their front hooves to scratch out wallows (p. 17), which may be 10 inches deep, in the soft earth. They urinate in the wallows and then roll in them as a part of their breeding ritual.

Social Interaction – Calves stay with the cow until she is ready to give birth the following spring. Bull moose are solitary. Two or three adults may feed together in the same meadow, but they seem to ignore each other.

Moose are quite vocal, especially during the breeding season. Cows emit a long, quivering moan which ends in a coughlike *mooo-agh*, which can be heard for 2 miles. Bulls respond with a deep, coarse grunt or bellow. Hunters imitate these sounds to call moose within shooting range.

Wyoming bull moose

Northwestern Canada bull moose

Cow with calf

Breeding – Beginning in September or October, bulls challenge each other for breeding rights to a cow in heat. Opponents rub trees, walk stiff-legged and sway their antlers to display dominance. Bulls of the same age and size often engage in violent antler battles, sometimes digging up the ground and toppling good-size trees. The victor breeds the cow repeatedly for 1 or 2 days, then moves on to breed other cows. In spring, young cows give birth to a single calf; older ones often have twins.

Habitat – Moose prefer brushy lowlands surrounded by conifer and hardwood forests. They are never far from swamps, lakes or rivers. In mountainous terrain, they live below the tree line, usually in thick willows. Moose also live on the fringes of agricultural land, provided it has suitable bedding and escape cover.

Food Habits – Moose leave their beds just before sunrise, browse for 2 or 3 hours and then move to nearby bedding thickets to rest and chew their cud. They feed again in late afternoon before bedding down for the night. Hunting pressure or other disturbances may force them to feed after dark. Shiras and Alaska-Yukon moose browse heavily on willows; Canada moose, on paper birch, quaking aspen and balsam fir. When desirable branches are too high, moose straddle the tree and walk forward to bend it over. In summer, they supplement their diet by eating aquatic plants.

Movement – Snow depths exceeding 3 feet restrict the movement of moose on high mountain slopes, forcing them into valleys. On flatter terrain, deep snow causes them to yard up along river banks or woodland openings. Most moose spend the entire year within a 5-square-mile area.

Bull moose feeding on aquatic plants

Because of their long legs, moose can easily stride over fallen trees and other obstacles. When alarmed, they crash through thick brush and small saplings without paying attention to trails. Moose can run up to 30 mph and swim across large lakes and rivers.

Population – Because the amount of moose habitat has remained stable in recent years, so have moose populations. Improved game management and enforcement practices have led to population growth in some areas. Moose sightings used to be rare in Minnesota, for instance, and there was no hunting season. But hunters now harvest several hundred moose each year.

Hunting Strategies – Stand-hunting is a good choice when moose are feeding in a particular swamp or using a well-worn trail. In areas laced with rivers and streams, try float-hunting. This way, you can easily surprise moose coming to drink or feed on aquatic plants.

The glass-and-stalk method works best in early morning, when moose are feeding in meadows and valleys. Be sure to finish your stalk before the animal retreats to bedding cover for the afternoon.

For maximum excitement, try calling or rattling. A cow-in-heat call or the sound of rattling antlers will draw rutting bulls into shooting range.

Trophy Records – Following are records for each of the moose categories recognized by the Boone and Crockett Club:

•Alaska-Yukon – 261$\frac{5}{8}$ points, with greatest outside spread of 65$\frac{1}{8}$ inches; shot in Fortymile River, Alaska, in 1994.

•Canada – 242 points, with a spread of 63 inches; taken in Grayling River, British Columbia, in 1980.

•Shiras – 205$\frac{4}{8}$ points, with a 53-inch spread; shot in Green River Lake, Wyoming, in 1952.

Eating Quality – Excellent. Moose meat is darker and slightly drier than beef.

BARREN GROUND CARIBOU bulls weigh 175 to 350 pounds. The antlers have very long main beams, numer- ous long points and a wide spread. Cows (inset) weigh 130 to 250 pounds and have short antlers with few points.

Caribou
(Rangifer tarandus)

Important Subspecies – Taxonomists disagree on the number of caribou subspecies, but the Boone and Crockett Club recognizes five types: mountain, woodland, barren ground, Central Canada barren ground, and Quebec-Labrador. Another variety, the Peary caribou, is a small whitish animal found only on the arctic islands.

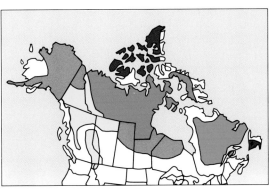

■Mountain ■Woodland ■Barren ground ■Central Canada Barren ground ■Quebec-Labrador ■Peary

Description – Caribou are unique in that both bulls and cows have antlers. Trophy bulls sport palmated antlers up to 5 feet long with large brow tines, or *shovels*, extending toward the nose. A cow's antlers are considerably smaller, rarely exceeding 2 feet in length.

Caribou have a brown or gray coat, with long, white hair, called a mane, from the throat to the chest. The neck and rump patch, and sometimes the belly and tip of the snout, are also white. Individuals from the same herd vary greatly in color.

The different types of caribou differ mainly in size and antler configuration (pp. 24 and 26).

Age and Growth – Calves weigh 9 to 12 pounds at birth. They grow to adult size in about 4 years. Bulls measure 6 to 7½ feet long and top out at 350 to 600 pounds, depending on the variety; cows weigh about 25 percent less. Caribou live up to 12 years.

Senses – Sense of smell, excellent; eyesight and hearing, fair. Caribou have difficulty detecting a motionless hunter, as long as he stays downwind.

Sign – Tracks (p. 119) are nearly round. Deeply rutted trails identify migration routes. Droppings are bell shaped and slightly concave on one end. Breath vapor given off by a huge herd may reveal their location, even when they're hidden behind a hill.

Social Interaction – Most of the year, caribou live in segregated bands of three types: bulls, yearlings of both sexes and cows with calves. The bond between cow and calf is very strong; if one is lost or killed, the other may spend days searching for it.

Before the spring and fall migration (p. 27), the bands join to form large herds. In mountainous regions, the herds usually number a few dozen; on the tundra, tens of thousands.

When migrating, caribou make belchlike grunts, probably to help keep track of each other. Calves make a high-pitched bawl when separated from the cow.

Breeding – Caribou mate in October and November, with breeding activity usually peaking during a 7- to 10-day period in mid- to late October. In large tundra herds, mature bulls trot back and forth through the column until they locate a cow in heat. In smaller mountain herds, bulls gather a harem of 10 to 15 cows, defending them from rival bulls until all of them have been bred.

In spring, when cows are ready to give birth, they move away from the herd to find a safe, isolated place in the rocky hills where they deliver 1 or 2 calves. Within an hour of birth, the calves are able to walk and follow the cow.

Habitat – Barren ground, Central Canada Barren ground, and Quebec-Labrador caribou live on the tundra – flat, open ground with permafrost beneath the mucky topsoil. The only plants are mosses, lichens, shrubs and dwarf conifers.

Mountain caribou live on steep, high-mountain slopes covered with conifers; woodland caribou, around bogs, rocky ridges and mountain foothills in heavily forested regions.

Food Habits – Caribou feed heavily in morning and late afternoon. Afterward, they look for an elevated spot to bed and chew their cud.

When on the tundra, caribou feed mainly on lichens, a virtually endless food source. In forested areas, they commonly eat cottongrass, horsetail, mushrooms and the leaves of willow, shrub birch and blueberry. In winter, caribou dig through the snow for greens or browse on small twigs.

MOUNTAIN CARIBOU. Largest of all caribou, the bulls weigh 400 to 600 pounds. Their heavily palmated antlers have very long points and a wide spread.

WOODLAND CARIBOU. Bulls weigh 300 to 400 pounds. The antlers usually have a narrow inside spread and the beams have a blunt end or very short points.

CENTRAL CANADA BARREN GROUND CARIBOU. Bulls weigh 175 to 350 pounds. The antlers are similar in shape to, but smaller than, those of barren ground caribou.

QUEBEC-LABRADOR CARIBOU. Bulls weigh 200 to 400 pounds. Their antlers have long points and the widest inside spread of all caribou.

Migrating caribou herd

Movement – The seasonal migrations of caribou are legendary. Tundra herds, usually led by bulls, travel up to 800 miles southward in fall to reach wintering areas that offer food. The migration stalls briefly during the breeding peak. In spring, pregnant cows lead the migration back to the summer range, where they give birth. Migrating herds normally travel 10 to 30 miles a day.

Mountain and woodland caribou do not migrate as far. In late fall, deep snow forces them off mountain slopes down to forested valleys. They move back up again in spring.

Caribou usually travel in an effortless trot, producing a characteristic clicking noise that results from the ankle tendons sliding over the leg bones. When disturbed, they can gallop at speeds up to 40 mph. Excellent swimmers, they can easily cross swift rivers on their migrations.

Population – Caribou populations appear to be stable under current game-management policies. Record book entries indicate no decline in the number of trophy bulls.

Hunting Strategies – On the tundra, hunters wait for migrating caribou along traditional trails, hiding behind boulders or brush. If you prefer the challenge of long-range shooting, however, find an elevated spot overlooking the trail. Prime spots along the trail include river crossings and necked-down areas between lake basins. In forested areas, still-hunt along the edges of open meadows and clearings. In mountainous or hilly terrain, try the glass-and-stalk technique.

Trophy Records – Following are the Boone and Crockett caribou records:

•Mountain *(right)* – 452 points, with an inside spread of $30\frac{3}{8}$ inches; shot in Turnagain River, British Columbia, in 1976.

•Woodland – $419\frac{5}{8}$ points, with a spread of $43\frac{2}{8}$ inches; taken in Newfoundland, prior to 1910.

•Barren ground – $465\frac{1}{8}$ points, with a spread of $40\frac{1}{8}$ inches; shot in Mosquito Creek, Alaska, in 1987.

•Central Canada barren ground – $433\frac{4}{8}$ points, with a spread of $40\frac{3}{8}$ inches; taken in Humpy Lake, Northwest Territories, in 1994.

•Quebec-Labrador – $474\frac{6}{8}$ points, with a spread of $58\frac{2}{8}$ inches; shot in Nain, Labrador, in 1931.

Eating Quality – Very good; the meat, which is similar to that of whitetail but drier, is a major food source for Indians and Eskimos.

Pronghorn
(Antilocapra americana)

Doe and kid

Common Names –
Antelope, pronghorn ante-
lope; unrelated to the true
antelopes of Africa and Asia.

Description – The name
"pronghorn" comes from the
sharp prongs that project
forward on the horns of the
buck. The horns differ from
those of other horned animals
in that the outer sheath is
shed each year. Mature bucks have horns that extend
above the ears. A doe may have buttons or spikes, but
they are shorter than the ears. The coat is a rich reddish tan above with white undersides, rump, cheeks
and neck patches. Bucks have distinct black cheek
patches and a broad black band on top of the snout.

Important Subspecies – Five types are currently
recognized: American, Oregon, Mexican, Peninsular,
and Sonoran pronghorns. The American pronghorn,
Antilocapra americana americana, is the most wide-
spread and abundant. Except for the Oregon pronghorn, which exists only in southeastern Oregon, the
remaining subspecies are found along the U.S.-Mexico
border and into central Mexico. The Peninsular and
Sonoran pronghorns are protected.

Age and Growth – At birth, *kids* weigh between 5
and 6 pounds. They reach adult size by age 3. Mature
bucks measure 4 to 5 feet in length and weigh 100 to
140 pounds. Females weigh about 20 percent less.
Pronghorns live up to 10 years.

Senses – Eyesight, excellent; sense of smell, very
good; hearing, good. The pronghorn's vision has been
compared to that of a human using 8X binoculars. A
doe in the herd will often stand guard, constantly
watching for approaching predators.

Sign – Tracks (p. 119) are often seen in the soft
ground near water holes. Droppings are similar to
those of mule deer. Pronghorns urinate and deposit
droppings in ground scrapes, which, unlike scrapes
of white-tailed deer, are made year-round and play
no role in breeding.

Social Interaction – Pronghorns are gregarious, living most of the year in groups of 5 to 40. The largest
bucks are often loners. In winters when food is
scarce, pronghorns may yard up in herds of more
than 100. They snort when surprised and flare the
white hair on their rump to alert others in the herd to
danger. Kids call adults with a high-pitched bleat.

American pronghorn buck

Breeding – Bucks often assemble a harem of up to
15 does, waging fierce battles to prevent other bucks
from breeding them. The dominant buck often runs
in circles, shakes his head side-to-side or jumps
wildly to interest a doe. Breeding takes place from
August to October and 1 to 3 kids are delivered in
late spring.

Habitat – Pronghorns are found on dry grasslands,
treeless foothills, brushlands, deserts and prairies.
They prefer rolling hills with coulees, river valleys
or water holes.

Food Habits – Primarily browsers, pronghorns do
most of their feeding in morning and late afternoon,
but they sometimes feed at night. Their favorite
foods include sagebrush, clover, alfalfa, cheatgrass,
wheatgrass and sedge.

Movement – When undisturbed, pronghorns usually
stay within a square mile. But they move much farther when food is in short supply or deep snow pre-
vents them from feeding. These movements are now
much shorter than they were in the past, however,
because of obstacles like fences and freeways.

Fastest of all North American game animals, pronghorns can run up to 60 mph. They seldom jump
fences, usually crawling under or between the wires.

Population – Stable throughout most of their range.

Hunting Strategies – Most pronghorns are taken
by the traditional glass-and-stalk method. During the
rut, you can often stalk to within a few hundred
yards of the herd, because the animals are preoccu-
pied with rutting displays. Another method rapidly
gaining in popularity, especially among bowhunters,
is decoying. Other effective techniques include
stand-hunting from ground pits or sitting in blinds
near water holes. A flat-shooting rifle with a high-
power scope is a must for most pronghorn hunting.

Trophy Records – The record pronghorn was shot
in Coconino County, Arizona, in 1985. The horns,
which scored $93\frac{4}{8}$ points, measured $17\frac{4}{8}$ and $17\frac{6}{8}$
inches in length, with base circumferences of 7 and
$6\frac{7}{8}$, and prong lengths of $8\frac{2}{8}$ and 8.

Eating Quality – Very good; the meat is similar to
that of mule deer, but finer in texture.

Mountain goat billy

Mountain Goat
(Oreamnos americanus)

Common Name – Rocky Mountain goat.

Description – Males, called *billies*, and females, called *nannies*, both have a humped back and a distinctive 4- to 5-inch beard. The creamy white coat sometimes has brown hairs on the back and rump. Both sexes have 8- to 11-inch horns that curve backward, but the billies' are thicker, with larger bases.

It may be difficult for a hunter to distinguish a billy from a nanny at long distance, but billies often have discolored fur on their belly. During the rut, they have a curious habit of sitting back on their haunches and pawing dirt onto their undersides.

Age and Growth – At birth, *kids* weigh about 7 pounds. They reach full size in 4 to 5 years, with billies measuring 5 to 6 feet in length and weighing 200 to 350 pounds. Nannies weigh only 100 to 200 pounds. Mountain goats live up to 12 years.

Senses – Eyesight, excellent; sense of smell and hearing, good.

Sign – The droppings are similar to those of mule deer. The squarish tracks (p. 119) are rarely seen on the rocky terrain.

Social Interaction – Nannies and kids live in groups of 2 to 10. Adult billies are usually loners, but when a billy lives in a nanny-kid group, nannies are dominant, except in the breeding season.

Mountain goats snort to warn each other of danger. Kids bleat if they become separated from the nanny.

Breeding – Billies competing for breeding rights may attempt to stab each other with their sharp horns, but they do not butt heads like sheep, because their horns and skulls are much more fragile. Mountain goats mate in November or December and the dominant billy stays with a nanny-kid group until all of the nannies have been bred. In spring, a nanny finds a cave or rugged area in the cliffs, where she delivers 1 to 3 kids.

Habitat – Found in some of the Rockies' most remote and rugged terrain, mountain goats can scale cliff faces so steep that they appear to defy gravity. They're usually found above the tree line at altitudes up to 8,000 feet.

Food Habits – Mountain goats feed from just before sunrise through midmorning and then bed near the feeding area to chew their cud. They feed again in late afternoon before bedding down for the night at a higher altitude, usually at the base of a rock.

Favorite summertime foods include grasses and forbs, such as wheatgrass and lupine. In winter, they browse on woody plants, such as balsam fir, willow and aspen. They eat mosses and lichens year-round, if they're available.

Movement – Deep snow forces mountain goats down to lower elevations in fall. They move back up when the snow melts in spring or, if high winds expose food, in winter.

When goats move along a rock face, they must carefully plan each step or risk plunging to their death. Their hooves are well adapted to the terrain, with spongy, cushioned bottoms that grip the rocks. Goats confronted with a dead-end path rise up on their hind feet, pivot toward the cliff face, set back down and go back the way they came. They use their front legs to help pull themselves up sheer cliffs, much like a human uses the rungs of a ladder.

Population – Stable, although numbers are modest. Unlike many big-game animals, goats have not lost habitat due to land development; in fact, they have

Nanny and kids

been successfully introduced in some mountainous areas where they were not native.

Hunting Strategies – The glass-and-stalk technique is the only practical method of taking a mountain goat. Begin by glassing for feeding animals in early morning. Once you spot a trophy, wait for it to bed down before beginning a stalk. Because mountain goats look downhill to detect danger, you must circle wide and try to get above them for a shot, which may take several hours. Don't shoot, however, if it looks like you won't be able to retrieve the animal, or you think it may tumble off a cliff.

Trophy Records – The record mountain goat, scoring 56⅝ points, was taken from the Babine Mountains, British Columbia, in 1949. Each horn measured 12 inches long, with a circumference of 6⅜ inches at the base.

Eating Quality – Good; the meat is similar in color and taste to pork, but tougher.

Dall's sheep ram

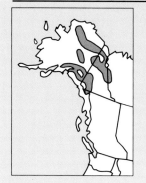

DALL'S SHEEP

- Pure white
- Rams weigh up to 220 pounds
- Found mainly in Alaska and the Yukon
- Almost always live above the tree line
- More migratory than Stone's sheep, continually moving from mountain to mountain

Thinhorn Sheep
(Including Dall's sheep and Stone's sheep)

Important Subspecies – Two are recognized: Dall's sheep, *Ovis dalli dalli*, also called white sheep, and Stone's sheep, *Ovis dalli stonei*.

Description – Dall's sheep are pure white, occasionally with black hairs on the tail. Stone's sheep vary in color from grayish white to black.

Stone's sheep ram

Rams have golden-colored horns that flare widely at the tips. Unlike bighorn rams, they have definite lengthwise ridges on the horns, and the tips are seldom *broomed*, or broken off. Ewes have spike-shaped horns that are usually less than 15 inches long.

Age and Growth – At birth, lambs average about 8 pounds. Dall's rams weigh 180 to 220 pounds; Stone's, up to 250. Both measure from 4½ to 6 feet long. Ewes weigh about 40 percent less than rams. Sheep live a maximum of 15 years. It takes about 8 years for a ram to develop full-curl horns (p. 35).

Senses – Eyesight, excellent; sense of smell and hearing, good. Sheep may not react to strange noises or smells until their eyes confirm the danger.

STONE'S SHEEP

- Grayish white to black
- Rams weigh up to 250 pounds
- Found mainly in the Yukon and British Columbia
- Normally live at or just below the tree line, but may venture above it
- Most reside on the same mountain throughout their life

Stone's sheep ewes with lambs

Sign – Tracks (p. 119) are similar to those of bighorn sheep and mountain goats. The dark brown droppings resemble those of mule deer.

Social Interaction – Animals of both sexes and all ages feed together in winter, because grazing area is limited. In spring, the herd splits up into two groups. One consists only of rams; the other, ewes, yearlings and lambs. Both groups have a leader, usually the oldest member. Lambs and ewes bleat to each other when separated.

Breeding – In November or December, rams begin searching for ewes in heat. The rams wage intense battles over breeding rights, rising up on their hind feet, lunging at each other and clashing horns. These clashes can be heard for miles.

Before breeding, the victorious ram tends a ewe in heat, making frequent deep blats. Rams mate with as many ewes as possible. In late spring, the ewes move to high-elevation rock ledges where they give birth to 1 or 2 lambs.

Habitat – Dall's sheep are found primarily in Alaska and the Yukon. They live above the tree line, usually at elevations of 2,500 feet or more. They prefer steep, open, alpine grasslands interrupted by rocky cliffs and shale slopes. Stone's sheep reside mainly in the Yukon and British Columbia. They're normally found at or just below the tree line on steep, rugged, isolated slopes covered by birch and fir thickets.

Food Habits – Both varieties have similar food habits. In summer, the diet includes locoweed, saxifrage, licorice root and other forbs; in winter, woody browse, such as crowberry, cranberry, sage and willow.

Sheep graze from predawn to midmorning, briefly at noon and again in late afternoon, resting to chew their cud in between. When they finish feeding for the day, they bed down at the base of a steep cliff.

Movement – In early fall, deep snow at high elevations makes travel difficult for sheep, covers most of their food and forces them down to south-facing slopes. After the snow melts in late spring, they move back to higher elevations. During summer, Dall's sheep continually move from mountain to mountain; Stone's sheep move considerably less.

Population – Stable; Dall's sheep are more plentiful than Stone's sheep.

World-record Stone's sheep

Hunting Strategies – Some hunters carry tents up the mountains, others set up a base camp in valleys and climb to high elevations each day. The most effective technique is to glass the slopes with a spotting scope to locate a trophy ram. The Dall's sheep's white coat usually stands out against the mountain, but Stone's sheep are more difficult to see, because they blend in with the rocky terrain. Once you spot the trophy you want, wait for it to bed down before beginning a stalk. For the best shot, try to get above the bedding site.

Trophy Records – Following are the Boone and Crockett Club records:

•Dall's – 189⁶⁄₈ points, with horns measuring 48⁵⁄₈ and 47⁷⁄₈ inches long; shot in Alaska's Wrangell Mountains, in 1961.

•Stone's – 196⁶⁄₈ points, with horns measuring 50¹⁄₈ and 51⁵⁄₈ inches long; taken in Muskwa River, British Columbia, in 1936. The only North American ram with 50-inch horns ever taken, it is widely regarded as the greatest of all big-game trophies.

Eating Quality – Excellent; the meat is leaner than beef, with no gamey flavor.

JUDGE the curl of a ram's horns as shown above. On a full curl, the tip of the horn reaches a line projecting from the rear base through the nostril. On a ¾ curl, the tip reaches a line projecting from the front base through the back of the eye. Most states and provinces define a legal ram as one having at least a ¾ curl; others, a full curl.

Rocky Mountain bighorn rams

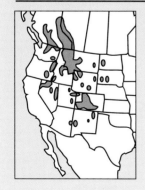

ROCKY MOUNTAIN BIGHORN

- Dark brown with relatively short ears and tail
- Rams weigh up to 300 pounds
- Usually found at elevations of 5,000 to 10,000 feet
- Feed primarily on grasses
- Migrate to lower elevations in late fall

Bighorn Sheep

(Including Rocky Mountain bighorns and desert bighorns)

Important Subspecies – Two main varieties: Rocky Mountain bighorn *(Ovis canadensis canadensis)* and desert bighorn *(Ovis canadensis nelsoni)*.

Description – Desert bighorns have longer, more pointed ears and a longer tail than Rocky Mountain bighorns. Rockies are usually dark brown; deserts, light brown. But coat color varies from dark to light in both types. The muzzle, rump patch and back of the legs are white; the belly, light tan. Rams have massive horns that are generally darker than

Ram with broomed horns

those of thinhorns and do not flare at the tips. The animals usually break off, or *broom,* the tips (above) to increase peripheral vision. A large ram's horns may weigh over 30 pounds. The short, slender horns of ewes never form more than a half curl.

Age and Growth – At birth, lambs weigh 8 to 9 pounds. Rams measure 5 to 6 feet long, with desert rams weighing 130 to 220 pounds; Rocky Mountains, 160 to 300. Ewes weigh one-half to two-thirds as much as rams. Bighorns grow full-curl horns in about 8 years and live up to 12.

Senses – Eyesight, excellent; sense of smell and hearing, good. Bighorns can spot a moving hunter more than a mile away.

Sign – Tracks (p. 119) are slightly larger, squarer and more closely spaced than those of mule deer. Beds, which are about 4 feet long and 6 to 12 inches deep, often smell of urine. The dark brown droppings resemble those of mule deer.

Social Interaction – Highly social animals, bighorns segregate into ram groups and ewe-lamb-yearling groups, just as thinhorns do. They also communicate the same way as thinhorns.

Breeding – Ewes come into heat from August to December, depending on latitude.

The heaviest-horned rams battle for dominance, clashing horns in the same manner as thinhorns.

Desert bighorn ram

Rocky Mountain ewe with lambs

DESERT BIGHORN

- Light brown, with relatively long ears and tail
- Rams weigh up to 220 pounds
- Usually found at elevations no greater than 5,000 feet
- Feed primarily on desert forbs
- No seasonal migration

The spectacular battle may last several hours, with the winner claiming breeding rights. He attempts to breed as many ewes as possible and often mounts the same one several times. If he leaves her side, however, she accepts a new mate. Ewes seek out a secluded cliffside where they give birth to 1 or 2 lambs in spring.

Habitat – Rocky Mountain bighorns inhabit the Rockies, from Alberta and British Columbia south to New Mexico. Normally found at elevations from 5,000 to 10,000 feet, they favor alpine meadows and grassy slopes below rugged, rocky cliffs.

Desert bighorns reside only in mountainous areas of the Desert Southwest, at altitudes from sea level up to 5,000 feet. At high elevations, they're usually found among juniper, pinyon pine and ponderosa pine; at low elevations, among desert plants, primarily cactus and yucca.

Food Habits – Bighorns feed in the morning and then rest in midday, usually on randomly chosen bedding sites on open ground, to chew their cud. They resume feeding in the afternoon before bedding down for the night at the base of a steep cliff protected from the wind.

Rocky Mountain bighorns graze primarily on wheatgrass, horsetail, pentstemon and June grass in summer; they browse on willow, alder and mountain mahogany in winter. Desert bighorns eat the same types of foods all year, relying mainly on grasses, such as galleta; forbs, like desert trumpet; and pulpy cactus centers.

Movement – Rocky Mountain bighorns spend summer and fall high in the mountains. After deep snow covers their food and makes it difficult to move about, they relocate to south-facing slopes, generally at altitudes of 2,000 to 5,000 feet. Desert bighorns do not move seasonally, but relocate as necessary to find an adequate water supply.

Population – Stable, but experts estimate that the bighorn's range is only about 5 percent of what it was a century ago, because of habitat loss.

Hunting Strategies – Most bighorn sheep hunters use the glass-and-stalk method. Begin by glassing at the base of a mountain, continuing until you cover the high country. Check every unusually shaped object, because sheep are difficult to see. When you spot a trophy ram, wait until it beds down before beginning your stalk, and then try to get above it for a shot.

Every serious sheep hunter wants to complete the "Grand Slam," by bagging all four kinds of bighorns and thinhorns. But you'll have to be extremely lucky

Rocky Mountain bighorns clashing horns

to draw a permit to hunt desert bighorns. Fish and game agencies in the U.S. issue less than 300 of them each year, with only about 30 going to nonresidents. In Mexico, permits are easier to obtain, but often very expensive. Preference is given to hunters who need only a desert bighorn to complete their grand slam.

Trophy Records – The Boone and Crockett Club lists the following records:

•Rocky Mountain bighorn – 208$\frac{1}{8}$ points; the horns, which measured 44$\frac{7}{8}$ and 45 inches in length, had base circumferences of 16$\frac{5}{8}$. The animal was shot in Blind Canyon, Alberta, in 1911.

•Desert bighorn – 205$\frac{1}{8}$ points; the horns measured 43$\frac{5}{8}$ and 43$\frac{6}{8}$ inches long, with base circumferences of 16$\frac{6}{8}$ and 17. The animal was shot in 1940 near the California-Mexico border.

Eating Quality – Excellent; the meat is leaner than beef with a mild flavor.

Bull bison

Bison
(Bison bison)

Common Names –
American bison, buffalo;
unrelated to the true buffalo
of Asia and Africa.

Description – Bison are the
largest hoofed mammal in
North America. But they
are very fast for their size,
capable of galloping up to
32 mph.

They have a huge, bearded
head, a humped back and two short, upturned horns.
The coat is dark brown to black, with long hair cov-

ering the head, neck, shoulders and front legs. Old
bulls may have light tan fur on their shoulders and
hump. Females have a smaller hump than males,
thinner horns and a shorter beard.

Important Subspecies – Two are recognized: the
Plains bison *(Bison bison bison)* and the wood bison
(Bison bison athabascae). The latter is larger and
darker in color. But these differences are not as distinct as they once were because of interbreeding
between the two.

Population – More than 60 million bison once
roamed the plains of North America. But heavy
hunting by white settlers and Indians reduced this
number to less than 1,000 by the year 1900.

Today, bison are confined to state or federal preserves
in the lower 48 states, but free-roaming herds are
still found in parts of Canada and Alaska. The North
American population is currently estimated at
190,000 to 200,000 animals.

Cow and calf

Age and Growth – At birth, calves weigh 40 to 50 pounds. They reach full size by age 5 or 6. Adult bulls measure 8½ to 10½ feet in length and weigh 900 to 2,000 pounds. Cows weigh 800 to 1,000 pounds. Bison live up to 20 years.

Senses – Sense of smell, good; eyesight and hearing, fair. Bison seldom use their senses to evade hunters or wolves, their only predators. Instead, they rely on their huge size and large herd numbers for defense, explaining why populations were so easily decimated by man.

Sign – Bison tracks (p. 119) and droppings look much like those of domestic cows. The droppings, called "buffalo chips," were an important source of fuel for early settlers. Bison dig wallows, 8- to 10-foot-wide depressions in the ground, and use them for taking dust or mud baths.

Social Interaction – Once found in herds of a million or more, bison are highly gregarious. Today's herds usually consist of 50 to 500 animals, with the largest numbering 7,500. Bison segregate into bull groups and cow-calf bands, each with 5 to 20 individuals.

Adults communicate by making a deep bellow; calves, a higher-pitched bawl. When nervous, bison paw at the ground or stamp their feet to alert others to danger.

Breeding – Breeding takes place from July to September. Bulls fight to establish dominance, charging each other and butting foreheads, but not clashing horns. In spring, cows give birth to 1 or 2 calves.

Habitat – Originally, bison were animals of the open plains. They have now adapted to many other habitat types, including river valleys, meadows, woodland openings and even coniferous forests.

Food Habits – Bison feed most heavily in early morning or late afternoon. They usually spend midday chewing their cud and taking dust baths.

Although they prefer to graze on wheat grass, bromegrass and wild rye, bison have adapted to browsing on woody plants. In winter, they paw through snow with their hooves or sweep it aside with their heads to uncover vegetation.

Movement – In the past, bison migrated up to 400 miles between summer and winter ranges to find food. These movements left trails that many modern highway systems now follow. Bison herds in Canada still migrate up to 150 miles.

Hunting Strategies – In Canada and Alaska, where there are open seasons, the majority of hunters use the glass-and-stalk technique. Hunting is allowed by lottery in a few states, and hunts are carefully controlled, often with only designated groups of bulls as legal game.

Trophy Records – The record bison was shot in Yellowstone National Park, Wyoming, in 1925. The horns, which scored 136⁴⁄8 points, measured 21²⁄8 and 23²⁄8 inches in length, with base circumferences of 16 and 15, and a greatest spread of 35³⁄8.

Eating Quality – Excellent; the meat is similar to beef, but leaner and slightly coarser.

Musk-Ox

(Ovibos moschatus)

Common Name – Arctic buffalo.

Description – The musk-ox is easily identified by its long, skirtlike coat, which hangs nearly to the ground. Most of the body is dark brown

to black; the lower legs and feet, white. In summer, the tips of the hair on the back turn blond from bleaching by the sun. Both sexes have broad, flat horns, but the bull's are nearly joined at the base and the cow's have enough space between them for hair to grow.

Age and Growth – Newborn calves weigh 23 to 33 pounds. They reach full size by age 4 or 5 and live up to 25 years. Bulls measure 7 to 8 feet long and weigh 575 to 900 pounds. Cows weigh 350 to 550.

Senses – Eyesight, excellent; sense of smell and hearing, good. Musk-oxen see very well during the winter in near-total darkness.

Sign – Tracks (p. 119) and droppings look much like those of domestic cattle. Deep trails in the snow may lead hunters to the animals.

Social Interaction – Mature bulls are generally loners; the rest of the animals live in herds of 5 to 20. Musk-oxen bellow deeply to alert others to danger; the sound may send the herd galloping away at speeds up to 25 mph. Or, they may form a *defensive line* (below), to intimidate predators.

Breeding – Several bulls join a herd and then battle for breeding rights by charging each other and clashing horns. In July or August, the dominant bull breeds all the herd's cows that are in heat. Cows usually breed every other year, and a single calf is born in spring.

Habitat – Found on the arctic tundra where temperatures commonly plunge below -60°F, musk-oxen spend the winter on windswept hilltops and slopes with exposed vegetation. In summer they prefer grassy river valleys, lakeshores and meadows.

Food Habits – Herds of these huge animals can quickly overgraze a pasture, so they move up to 15 miles a day to find food. They feed any time of day, pausing only briefly to rest and chew their cud. In summer, they graze on grasses, sedges and forbs, such as willow herb and knotweed. In winter, they browse on shrubs, such as ground birch and willow.

Movement – Musk-oxen may move up to 50 miles in winter to find feeding areas blown free of snow.

Population – In the late 1800s, musk-oxen were hunted to near extinction for their hides and meat. Hunting is now carefully controlled, and the North American population exceeds 60,000.

Hunting Strategies – Hunters must be prepared for extremely severe winter conditions, even though the hunts are in spring and fall. Most outfitters provide wall tents and equip their guests with the caribou or sealskin clothing traditionally worn in the Arctic.

The hunt, which typically takes a week or more, begins by glassing from a snowmobile to locate a trophy bull. Once you spot the animal, the law requires you to hunt on foot for the last mile. During the stalk, you can conceal yourself behind boulders and snowdrifts.

Trophy Records – The record musk-ox was shot in Bay Chimo, Northwest Territories, in 1988. The horns, which scored $125\frac{2}{8}$ points, measured $27\frac{2}{8}$ and $27\frac{1}{8}$ inches in length, and had a greatest spread of $30\frac{4}{8}$ inches.

Eating Quality – Good, but a little darker and much drier than beef.

Defensive line

Musk-ox cow (left) and bull (right)

Javelina
(Tayassu tajacu)

Common Name – Collared peccary. Incorrectly called wild hog or wild pig by many hunters, javelina do not belong to the wild pig family and have no close relatives in North America.

Description – Javelina have short, bristly, slate-gray to black hair with whitish tips. They can erect their long neck hair to form a mane. The name "collared peccary" comes from the whitish ring around the neck.

The sexes look alike; both have 2-inch-long upper and lower tusks, which fit together so closely that they sharpen each other to a razorlike edge.

Age and Growth – Javelina weigh about 1 pound at birth, reaching full size within a year and living up to 15. Adults in the northern part of the range measure 3 feet long and weigh 30 to 50 pounds. Those in the southern part weigh about 15 percent less.

Senses – Sense of smell, excellent; hearing, good; eyesight, very poor. They use their sense of smell to find food buried as much as 6 inches below ground.

Sign – Tracks (p. 119) are often seen on the soft ground near water holes. Feeding sign includes ripped-up prickly pear cactus and rooted-up areas in the ground.

Social Interaction – Javelina live in herds of 5 to 30 animals of various ages and both sexes. Sows out-rank boars in the herd's dominance order. The entire herd moves, feeds and rests together.

Herd members keep track of each other with soft grunts and, when threatened, make barklike warning coughs. The musk gland on the back emits an odor that is unique for each individual.

Breeding – Javelina mate any time of the year, producing a single annual litter. Boars do not compete for breeding rights, and a sow in heat accepts many partners. No prolonged boar-sow relationship ever develops. About 20 weeks after breeding, the sow delivers 1 to 4 young.

Javelina feeding on prickly pear cactus

Sow and young

Habitat – Found in brushy deserts, rocky canyons, scrub oak forests and arid mountain foothills, usually at elevations of 1,500 feet or less. But in parts of Arizona and New Mexico, javelina live at altitudes up to 6,000 feet among Mexican gray oaks and scattered junipers.

Food Habits – Javelina feed in early morning and late evening, bedding down in thickets during the midday heat.

Their favorite food is cactus, primarily prickly pear. They also eat berries, fruits, nuts, roots, insects, bird eggs, mice and rats. Contrary to popular belief, they do not compete with domestic grazing animals for food.

Movement – Javelina spend most of their life in an area of no more than 5 square miles. They do not migrate seasonally, but may move 10 to 20 miles if there is a shortage of food or water. Javelina run with a stiff-legged gallop and have been clocked at 25 mph.

Population – Stable throughout most of the range.

Hunting Strategies – In desert and low mountain terrain, hunters glass with binoculars to spot javelina moving in and out of draws, and then stalk to within shooting range. Because of their poor eyesight, you can easily approach them from downwind.

An effective technique in the brush country of southern Texas is stand-hunting in morning or evening next to water holes or along *sendaros*, bulldozed trails used in farming or oil exploration.

Trophy Records – No official record, but animals weighing up to 65 pounds have been taken.

Eating Quality – Very good; the light-colored meat is dry in texture and best when roasted.

Wild Boar
(Sus scrofa)

Piglets nursing

Common Names – Wild pig, wild hog, razorback.

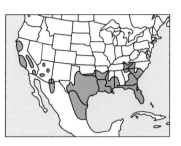

History – Native to Europe and Asia, the wild boar was introduced to North America in 1893, when 50 boars from Germany were released on a New Hampshire hunting preserve. Introductions continued well into the 1900s, and today's populations are centered around these release sites. No other type of wild pig exists in North America.

Description – Wild boar are easily identified by their 5- to 9-inch upper tusks and erect 4- to 5-inch ears. Both sexes are nearly identical in appearance. The long, bristly coat is usually black, but may be brown or gray. Adults develop a thick mane and their hair has blond-colored tips.

Age and Growth – *Piglets* weigh 1 to 2 pounds at birth but grow rapidly, reaching adult size by age 3. Males measure 4 to 6 feet in length and weigh 300 to 400 pounds. Females weigh about 25 percent less. Wild boar live up to 15 years.

Senses – Sense of smell, very good; hearing, good; eyesight, poor. Wild boar use their sense of smell to find food, even that which is underground.

Sign – Tracks (p. 119) resemble those of domestic hogs. Often, you'll see rooting on the forest floor, where wild boar have been digging for food. Droppings look like a string of sausage links. Beds, usually found in secluded thickets, consist of a pile of grass and twigs.

Social Interaction – Sows and piglets live in family groups of about 6; several groups may merge to form a herd of 50 or more. Boars usually live alone, but several may band together. Wild boar communicate by making grunts and squeals similar to those of a domestic hog.

Breeding – Mating takes place in December or January, with boars traveling between family groups to find receptive sows. If a sow is not bred during the 2 or 3 days she is in heat, she will come into heat again 21 days later. A litter usually consists of 4 to 6 piglets, but may number up to 14.

Habitat – Capable of adapting to practically any kind of habitat, wild boar are most commonly found in swamps, brushlands, woodlands and mountain forests.

Food Habits – Wild boar feed heavily at dawn and dusk; they spend hot afternoons rolling in mud wallows to cool down and avoid insects. Their diet includes acorns, hickory and beech nuts, roots, corn, berries, crayfish, frogs, young rabbits and even fawns.

Movement – Wild boar live in an area of 10 square miles or less, but they may cover up to 50 square miles when food is in short supply. They can gallop up to 30 mph.

Population – Although populations are expanding, hybrids, the result of wild boar breeding with domestic hogs, account for much of the increase. Hunters often oppose new introductions, because wild boar compete with deer and other game animals for food. Farmers also oppose them, because the boars' excessive rooting can severely damage crops.

Hunting Strategies – One of the most effective methods is driving heavy cover with hounds, pushing boar down escape routes to waiting posters. You can also still-hunt, moving slowly and silently through known feeding areas, doing more looking than walking. Or, you can stand-hunt near feeding areas, waiting for boar to come to you.

For regulation purposes, most states do not distinguish between wild boar, hybrids, which are not as hairy, and *feral pigs*, which are domestic hogs that have escaped or were released into the wild.

Trophy Records – No official record, but animals approaching 600 pounds have been taken.

Eating Quality – Excellent; the meat is much like domestic pork, but considerably tastier.

Carnivores

Order Carnivora

Carnivores, or flesh eaters, have four long canine teeth used for seizing and killing prey. Some, such as black bear, are *omnivorous*, eating berries, nuts and fruits in addition to animal flesh. Carnivores also have strong claws used for digging, grasping and fighting.

This order includes the largest, most powerful big-game animals in North America, such as the brown bear and polar bear, which reach weights approaching a ton. Many of these animals are highly unpredictable and, in certain instances, extremely dangerous.

Besides bears, which many consider the ultimate big-game trophy, the order includes other animals sought by big-game hunters, such as wolves and mountain lions, and smaller game, like raccoon, bobcat and fox.

Most carnivores remain active year-round, but bears and raccoons spend winter in a semidormant state. However, they do not hibernate in the true sense, because their body temperature remains almost normal, and they immediately awaken and move about when disturbed.

Carnivores usually have one litter annually, and the offspring require extended parental care. Before the young establish their own territories, the parents teach them to be successful hunters.

Grizzly bear

48

Black bear – dark brown phase

Black bear – cinnamon phase

Black Bear

(Ursus americanus)

Common Names – None; dark-brown phase black bears are mistakenly called brown bears or grizzlies.

Description – Black bears exhibit many different color phases, with black being by far the most common, followed by dark brown, cinnamon and blond. Some subspecies may even be bluish

Black bear – black phase

or white. Both sexes have a tan muzzle, small black eyes, rounded ears, a 4-inch tail and 1¼-inch claws, which enable them to climb trees – something no other North American bear can do. Many black bears have a V-shaped patch of white hair on the chest.

Important Subspecies – Common varieties include: the eastern black bear, *Ursus americanus americanus*, found from the Rocky Mountains to the eastern seaboard, and the less numerous cinnamon bear, *Ursus americanus cinnamomum*, found mainly in British Columbia. The former is the most likely to be black, the latter is just as likely to be cinnamon-colored as black.

Age and Growth – At birth, *cubs* weigh 6 to 12 ounces. They grow to full size in 4 to 6 years and may live up to 20. An adult boar normally measures 4½ to 6 feet long and weighs 250 to 375 pounds; exceptionally large ones may exceed 600. Sows usually weigh 150 to 200 pounds.

Senses – Senses of smell and hearing, excellent; eyesight, poor. Black bears depend on their sense of

Ripped-open stump

Claw marks   *Trails*   *Droppings*

smell to locate food. They have difficulty detecting a motionless hunter, as long as he stays downwind.

Sign – Tracks (p. 120) are most commonly found in the mud along riverbanks, lakeshores and the edges of swamps. Droppings, which contain bits of berries, nuts, hair, grass, insects and even fish scales, help hunters determine what the bears have been eating. Ripped-open rotten stumps show where bears are feeding on insects or searching for honey. Claw marks on trees mark a bear's territory, and the scratching sharpens the claws. Well-worn trails wind through tall grassy areas.

Social Interaction – Sows stay with their cubs (right), but boars live alone, except during the breeding season. Bears often congregate in prime feeding areas, such as garbage dumps, but they seem to ignore each other.

Black bear cubs make a muffled whine when separated from the sow, and all adults growl or snort to intimidate a foe.

Breeding – Prior to breeding, boars travel great distances to find the scent trail of a sow in heat. Sows may mate with more than one boar and, if two similar-size boars find her at the same time, they fight for breeding rights. Breeding takes place in early summer, but a sow mates only in alternate years. She gives birth to 1 to 5 cubs in midwinter and fiercely protects them for 1 or 2 years, until they can survive on their own.

Habitat – Black bears prefer thick, unbroken woodlands with an abundance of wet lowlands and heavy growths of ferns, shrubs and tall grasses. They're also found on forested mountains, but they do not adapt well to agricultural areas.

Sow with cub

Black bear at bait site

Food Habits – True omnivores, black bears eat many types of fruits and berries; farm crops, such as corn and oats; honey; insects; fish; nuts; garbage and carrion.

When food is plentiful, black bears feed at sunrise, sunset and through the night, spending the afternoon bedding in thickets near feeding sites. When food is scarce, they forage over a much larger area, moving and feeding any time of the day or night. The largest boars feed almost exclusively after dark.

Movement – Boars establish territories of up to 100 square miles and defend them from all other bears. Sows have much smaller territories, which they share with juveniles but defend from adults.

Black bears spend the winter months hibernating in their den, which may be a small cave dug into a hillside, the cavity in a hollow tree or a nook inside a brush pile. They also winter in culverts under roads and foundations of abandoned buildings.

While hibernating, their body temperature drops slightly and their metabolism slows, but not nearly as much as that of many rodents, such as woodchucks. They may even awaken and leave their dens during a warm spell. In cold climates, they stay in their dens from October to May; in milder climates, from January to March.

Although black bears usually lumber along slowly, they are capable of much higher speeds and may run up to 30 mph when disturbed.

Population – Stable throughout most of the range. Because individual black bears require such large territories, overpopulation is seldom a problem.

Hunting Strategies – Baiting (above) is the most widely used hunting technique. To select a bait site, look for areas where bears have been feeding naturally, as indicated by their droppings.

If legal, start baiting on a daily basis 2 or 3 weeks before the hunting season. Dig a large pit upwind of your tree stand, and fill it with such items as meat scraps, sweet corn, watermelon, honey, pastries or molasses mixed with oats.

When the hunting season arrives, sneak into your stand in early afternoon and wait for a bear to come in. It will usually show up during the last 2 hours of daylight. If you were to go out in early morning, you'd spook any bear near the bait and it would probably not return that day.

In some states, hunters are allowed to use specially trained hounds to trail and tree black bears. The hunter finds a treed bear by the sound of the hounds' wailing, and then elects to shoot it or let it go.

Trophy Records – The record black bear was found dead in San Pete County, Utah, in 1975. The skull, which scored $23^{10}/16$ points, measured $14^{12}/16$ inches long and $8^{14}/16$ inches wide.

Eating Quality – Good; the meat is much like beef, but coarser and darker, with a gamier taste.

Alaskan brown bear

ALASKAN BROWN BEAR

- Maximum weight 1,600 pounds
- Moderate-length claws
- Restricted to coastal areas near salmon spawning streams
- Feeds mainly on salmon

Alaskan Brown & Grizzly Bear
(Ursus arctos)

Important Subspecies – Two are officially recognized: the Alaskan brown bear, *Ursus arctos middendorffi*, found along Pacific coastal areas and islands of Alaska and British Columbia, and the smaller grizzly bear, *Ursus arctos horribilis*, which inhabits parts of Alaska, western Canada, the Northwest Territories, Montana, Idaho and Wyoming.

Silvertip and brown-phase (inset) grizzly bears

Common Name – Alaskan browns from Kodiak Island, Alaska, are usually called Kodiak bears.

Description – Alaskan browns and grizzlies can be easily distinguished from black bears by the prominent hump above the shoulders and the longer claws. Grizzlies have even longer claws than Alaskan browns. The coat is normally dark brown, but some grizzlies, called *silvertips,* have blond-tipped hair on the back, sides and head. The sexes are nearly identical in appearance.

Age and Growth – At birth, cubs weigh 12 to 24 ounces. They grow to full size by age 7 or 8 and live up to 30 years. Grizzly boars normally measure 6 to

GRIZZLY BEAR

- Maximum weight 1,100 pounds
- Long claws
- Range extends farther inland than that of Alaskan brown
- Feeds mainly on berries and freshly killed mammals

Grizzly cubs nursing

Alaskan brown fishing at waterfall

8 feet long and weigh 500 to 800 pounds, but may reach 1,100. Alaskan brown boars measure 8 to 10 feet long, weigh 800 to 1,200 pounds and occasionally reach 1,600. Sows of both varieties weigh about one-third less than boars.

Senses – Sense of smell, excellent; hearing, good; eyesight, poor.

Sign – The tracks (p. 120), usually found along rivers and lakeshores, are much larger than those of black bears; claw marks on trees, which mark an individual's territory, are higher off the ground. Trails up to 10 inches deep connect preferred bedding and feeding spots. The cylindrical droppings are laced with bits of fruit, grass, fish scales and whatever else the animals have been eating. Feeding sign includes conifer trees stripped of the outer bark, and diggings, where bear have unearthed roots or ground squirrel colonies.

Social Interaction – Adults are solitary, but immatures, from age 2 to 5, often live in pairs. Cubs stay with the sow for up to 2 years. She protects them from other bears by snarling and charging violently.

Alaskan browns, however, fight to establish dominance when feeding in large groups along salmon rivers (opposite). Standing on their hind legs, they attempt to bite their opponent or lash out at it with their claws. Old bears generally have deep scars resulting from these vicious battles.

An angry bear growls, woofs or snaps its teeth to drive off other bears that enter its feeding area or threaten its cubs. Lost cubs whine or whimper to call the sow.

Breeding – Prior to breeding in late spring to mid-summer, a boar courts a sow for about 2 weeks. They sleep together, feed together and frequently nuzzle each other. Sometimes, two boars of equal size court and breed the same sow. After breeding, the boar abandons her and searches for another sow. The sow breeds only every other year. The litter, which normally numbers 2 but occasionally includes 4, is delivered in the den in mid- to late winter.

Habitat – Grizzlies are found on the tundra, in woodlands and on mountain foothills. Ideal habitat has a mixture of open meadows, forest edges and brushy lakeshores or streambanks. In the U.S., grizzlies are confined mainly to National Parks.

Alaskan browns are found along coastal areas, usually near salmon spawning rivers or smaller streams and lakes connected to them. They prefer dense cover, such as willow thickets or tall grass.

Food Habits – These bears feed any time of the day or night. They convert to night feeding, however, when humans are present. When food is in short supply, the bears scour the landscape, covering as much as 100 square miles. They move much less when food is plentiful, spending more of their time resting in heavy cover near feeding sites.

Alaskan browns fighting

A grizzly's diet depends on time of year. In spring, they eat grasses, roots, insects, mice and carrion; in summer, berries and large mammals, such as elk, moose, mountain sheep, black bear and even cattle. If they can't finish the animal in one sitting, they cover it with sticks and return later. In fall, they dig up hibernating rodents, such as marmots and ground squirrels.

Alaskan browns have similar feeding habits, but they spend the summer feeding on salmon. A few dozen bears may gather at a spawning river, with some chasing salmon in shallow pools and others catching them in midair at waterfalls (opposite).

Grizzlies digging up rodents

Movement – Grizzly and Alaskan brown bears spend their lives in an area of about 8 to 10 square miles, unless a food shortage forces them to range more widely. Like black bears, they winter in dens. Surprisingly fast for their size, they can run up to 30 mph.

Population – Stable; grizzly populations declined dramatically in the last century, because of habitat loss, shortage of prey and indiscriminate killing. But hunting is now carefully controlled, and grizzlies in the U.S. are protected. Alaskan browns are not as closely associated with humans, so their population has not undergone a similar decline.

Hunting Strategies – Most hunters use the glass-and-stalk technique. Climb to an elevated spot so you can glass the open meadows below. After spotting a trophy bear, approach it from downwind so it can't smell you, and stalk to within shooting range. Regulations require that nonresidents hunt grizzlies and Alaskan browns with a guide.

Trophy Records – The record Alaskan brown bear scored $30^{12}/_{16}$ points and was shot on Kodiak Island, Alaska, in 1952. The skull measured $17^{15}/_{16}$ inches long and $12^{13}/_{16}$ inches wide.

Three animals are tied for the grizzly bear record with a score of $27^{2}/_{16}$ points.

Eating Quality – Fair; similar to black bear, but gamier. The best-tasting meat comes from animals that were eating berries, rather than fish or carrion.

Polar Bear
(Ursus maritimus)

Description – Largest of the North American game animals, the polar bear may reach a weight of 2,200 pounds. Both sexes have a creamy white coat, a long neck and sharp 3-inch claws, used for killing prey and gripping ice.

Age and Growth – Polar bears weigh 1 to 2 pounds as newborn cubs, grow to full size in 5 to 7 years and live up to 30. Males normally measure 7 to 11 feet long and weigh 900 to 1,600 pounds; females weigh about 30 percent less.

Senses – Sense of smell, excellent; hearing and eyesight, very good. Polar bears can smell dead seals up to 10 miles away. They can hear live seals swimming and barking below the ice.

Sign – Tracks (p. 120) in deep, soft snow are usually the only visible sign. The presence of arctic fox, which feed on seal carcasses partially eaten by bears, means bears are in the area.

Social Interaction – Polar bears are loners, except during the breeding season or when feeding at a dump or on a large carcass. Cubs stay with the sow for about 2½ years, until she is ready to breed again. When angry, polar bears growl and hiss. The cubs whine if separated from the sow.

Breeding – In early spring, a boar may travel hundreds of miles to find a receptive sow. Boars wage bloody, occasionally fatal, battles for breeding rights, slashing each other with their front claws. Like grizzly boars, they court the female for about 2 weeks before breeding, and then move on to mate with another sow. One to three cubs are born in the den in midwinter.

Habitat – Polar bears live on the arctic coast of North America and on arctic islands and ice floes. They prefer broken floes for hunting seals and avoid solidly frozen ice.

Food Habits – Polar bears travel as much as 60 miles a day in search of food and may feed at any time of the day or night. In spring and fall, they kill seals and young walruses and scavenge beached whale carcasses. In summer, the diet includes grasses, seaweed, berries, mice, bird eggs, crabs and fish.

Movement – In the northern part of their range, polar bears ride the ice floes all year. But in Hudson Bay, many bears ride the floes up to 400 miles south in spring and, when the ice melts in summer, migrate back north along the coastline. In fall, polar bears make dens in snowbanks along hillsides or beneath chunks of broken ice along pressure ridges. Females may spend nearly half the year in the den, entering in late fall, giving birth and nurturing the cubs and emerging in spring. Males spend only about 2 months in the den, leaving in midwinter.

Fast for their size, polar bears can run up to 25 mph and swim nonstop for 50 miles at speeds up to 6 mph. They can submerge under the ice for up to 2 minutes.

Population – Stable; as human presence in the Arctic increased, overharvesting for hides and shooting of problem bears caused the population to plummet. But strict game laws have stopped the decline.

Hunting Strategies – Polar bear hunts are extremely expensive and physically demanding, requiring you to spend a week or more on the ice pack, living in an igloo or tent with an Eskimo guide. Each day, you travel by dog sled to the broken edge of the ice pack and then find a high vantage point on a snowdrift or pressure ridge. After locating a trophy bear with a spotting scope, you stalk on foot, sometimes several miles, to get close enough for a shot. On fresh snow, you may be able to track polar bear to within shooting distance.

Trophy Records – The record polar bear was shot in Kotzebue, Alaska, in 1963. The skull, which scored $29^{15}/_{16}$ points, measured $18^{8}/_{16}$ inches long and $11^{7}/_{16}$ inches wide.

Eating Quality – Fair; the meat, eaten regularly by Eskimos, is similar to that of brown bears. But the liver is poisonous, due to the high vitamin A concentration.

Sow with cub

Mountain Lion

(Felis concolor)

Female with kittens

Common Names – Cougar, puma, catamount, panther.

Description – Mountain lions are easily distinguished from other cats by their small, rounded ears and 3-foot-long, brown-tipped tails. Both sexes have unspotted coats that are usually light brown, but may be reddish brown, yellowish or grayish.

Age and Growth – At birth, *kittens* weigh $1/2$ to 1 pound. They are full grown in about 2 years and live up to 15. Adult males measure 7 to $9\frac{1}{2}$ feet long from nose to tip of tail and weigh 140 to 175 pounds. Females weigh about one-third less.

Senses – Eyesight and night vision, excellent; senses of smell and hearing, good. Mountain lions can see well enough to hunt in near-total darkness. They feel their way through dense thickets with the help of their sensitive whiskers.

Sign – The tracks (p. 121) are commonly found in the dirt at the mouths of caves, around desert springs or in fresh snow. The claws retract, so they do not show in the tracks. Mountain lions scratch the ground with their front feet to make dirt mounds and then urinate on the mounds to mark their territories. They hide their droppings, which contain hairs and bits of bone, by covering them with dirt and twigs.

Social Interaction – Mountain lions are solitary, establishing individual territories. Females raise the young for 1 or 2 years and teach them to hunt. The animals growl or hiss to drive off a strange cat or defend a kill. Kittens make a mewing sound when separated from the female; she answers with a soft grunt.

Breeding – Males follow the scent of a female in heat, and several may fight for breeding rights by slashing each other with their front claws. The winner breeds her for about 2 weeks, and then leaves to find another female in heat. About 3 months later, the female finds an uprooted tree, dense thicket or rocky depression, where she delivers 1 to 3 kittens.

Female mountain lions, unlike the females of other North American cats, come into heat once a month and may give birth any time of the year. But they have a litter only every 2 or 3 years.

Habitat – Found in forested foothills and high mountain slopes, rocky canyons, desert thickets and densely vegetated swamps from western Canada southward through Mexico and South America. Mountain lions may live above the tree line, at elevations up to 13,000 feet.

Food Habits – Primarily night feeders, mountain lions may travel more than 20 miles on their nightly hunts. They spend the day resting on high, rocky ledges.

Mountain lions eat a wide variety of animals, ranging in size from shrews to moose, but mule deer comprise most of their diet. They occasionally take livestock. They stalk to within 30 feet of large prey before attacking. If they can't eat their kill in one sitting, they cover it with branches and return later.

Movement – Mountain lions normally live within a 15- to 40-square-mile territory, but in areas where mule deer and other prey make seasonal shifts, the cats follow close behind. They can sprint up to 30 mph and make 15-foot vertical leaps.

Population – Stable or increasing over much of the range. In some areas where hunting is not permitted, mountain lion populations have increased to the point where attacks on humans and livestock are becoming too frequent.

Hunting Strategies – Hunters use specially trained hounds to track mountain lions, usually on fresh snow. The hunts may last several days or even weeks, because the cats may travel dozens of miles through rugged country when pursued. Once the dogs tree a cat, hunters assess its trophy potential and then make the decision on whether to shoot it or let it go.

Trophy Records – The record mountain lion was shot in Tatlayoko Lake, British Columbia, in 1979. The skull, which scored $16^4/16$ points, measured $9^9/16$ inches long and $6^{11}/16$ inches wide.

Eating Quality – Fair. Mountain lions are hunted as trophies; the dry meat is seldom eaten.

Bobcat
(Lynx rufus)

Common Names – Wildcat, bay lynx.

Description –  Named for its short tail, which appears to be bobbed, the bobcat is North America's most common wild cat. Both sexes are yellowish brown above and white below, with dark brown or black spots and bars. The tail has narrow black stripes with a wide black band near the end and a white tip. The ears have black tufts that are shorter than those of the lynx.

Age and Growth – Weighing 4 to 8 ounces at birth, kittens grow to full size in 2 years and live up to 15. Males measure 32 to 44 inches from head to tip of tail and weigh 15 to 30 pounds. Females weigh about 20 percent less.

Senses – Eyesight and night vision, excellent; hearing, good; sense of smell, fair. Bobcats can spot the slightest movement, even in near-total darkness.

Sign – Scratch marks on tree trunks show where bobcats have been sharpening their claws. Like mountain lions, they make dirt mounds and urinate on them to mark their territory. They also cover their droppings, which resemble those of domestic dogs, with dirt and twigs, so they're difficult to find. The tracks (p. 121) are seldom seen, except on soft snow.

Social Interaction – Male bobcats are solitary; females spend most of the year with the young, teaching them to stalk and kill prey. Like domestic cats, bobcats communicate by making meows, hisses and purrs.

Breeding – Males begin yowling in late winter to advertise their presence to females. After mating, the male leaves immediately to find other females in heat. The litter, delivered in spring, includes from 1 to 7 kittens. A second litter is possible in the southern part of the range.

Habitat – Highly adaptable, bobcats can live practically anywhere, with the exception of urban areas or land that is intensively farmed. Ideal habitat for the cats consists of woodlands or mountain foothills with an abundance of thickets, which provide cover for stalking prey.

Food Habits – Bobcats do most of their hunting at night, when their prey is most active, but they may hunt anytime. After gorging itself on a kill, a cat usually rests for a day or two in a hollow log or rock crevice.

Their diet consists mainly of rabbits and hares, but they also eat squirrels, mice, rats, ground-nesting birds, porcupines and even turkeys roosting in trees. Like mountain lions, they cover whatever they cannot finish and come back for it later.

Movement – Bobcats normally hunt in a 10- to 30-square-mile territory. But they roam more widely when the food supply dwindles. When chasing prey, they can run 25 to 30 mph.

Population – Stable throughout most of the range. Populations have rebounded in most areas where bounty hunting was once practiced.

Hunting Strategies – Most hunters use dogs to track and tree the cats, which are killed for their pelts. You can also draw bobcats into shooting range by using a call that sounds like an injured rabbit.

Trophy Records – No official record, but a male bobcat shot in Colorado in 1951 weighed 69 pounds.

Eating Quality – Fair. Bobcats are hunted for their pelts; the tough, dry meat is seldom eaten.

Lynx
(Lynx lynx)

Common Name –
Canada lynx.

Description – Lynx
are easily distin-
guished from bobcats
by their longer ear
tufts, larger feet and
shorter tail, which
lacks black stripes

and has a black band covering the entire tip. Both
sexes are grayish to reddish brown with faint black
spots and bars and light brown undersides.

Important Subspecies – Two are recognized: the
Canada lynx, *Lynx lynx canadensis*, which inhabits
much of Canada and parts of the western U.S.; and the
Newfoundland lynx, *Lynx lynx subsolanus*, a slightly
smaller, darker animal, found only on that island.

Age and Growth – Newborn kittens weigh 8 to 10
ounces and grow to full size in about 2 years. Adult
males measure 34 to 40 inches from head to tip of
tail and weigh 22 to 35 pounds; females weigh about
25 percent less. Lynx live up to 15 years.

Senses – Eyesight, night vision and hearing, excellent; sense of smell, fair. Like bobcats, lynx have
superb ability to spot movement at night.

Sign – Tracks (p. 121) are exceptionally large for the
animal's size and may be confused with those of the
mountain lion. Scratches on trees show where lynx
have been sharpening their claws. They bury their
droppings in the same manner as mountain lions.

Lynx kitten

Social Interaction – The social behavior of lynx is nearly identical to that of bobcats, with males living by themselves and females tending the young. They also communicate in much the same way as bobcats.

Breeding – Mating habits are similar to those of bobcats, with the male breeding the female for a few days and then moving on to breed others. She has a litter of 1 to 5 kittens in early spring, usually in a den beneath an uprooted tree.

Habitat – Found in dense forested areas with an abundance of windfalls, swamps and brushy thickets, lynx require heavy cover for concealment when stalking prey. In the northern part of their range, they venture onto the tundra when food becomes scarce.

Food Habits – Lynx do most of their hunting after dark but, on occasion, hunt early or late in the day. In midday, they rest in hollow logs, under low branches or at the base of rock ledges.

A lynx's diet consists mainly of snowshoe hares, squirrels, chipmunks, mice and ground-nesting birds. But they occasionally kill the young of deer, wild sheep and even caribou.

Movement – When small animals are plentiful, lynx require less than 10 square miles for hunting. But in years when food is scarce, they may follow migrating deer or caribou as far as 100 miles. Lynx can sprint up to 20 mph, but tire quickly.

Population – Cyclical, with peaks about every 10 years, matching those of snowshoe hares.

Hunting Strategies – Techniques used for hunting bobcat are equally effective for lynx.

Trophy Records – No official record, but lynx have been known to reach 42 pounds.

Eating Quality – Fair. Lynx are hunted for their pelts; the meat is tough and seldom eaten.

Gray Wolf
(Canis lupus)

Common Names –
Timber wolf, lobos,
tundra wolf.

Description – The
coat of both sexes is
usually gray, but the
color varies from all
white to all black,
sometimes within the same litter. Wolves are easily
distinguished from coyotes by their larger size.

Important Subspecies – The two major varieties
are: the northern Rocky Mountain wolf, *Canis lupus
occidentalis*, a large wolf that inhabits Alaska and
most of western Canada; and the eastern timber
wolf, *Canis lupus nubilus*, which is slightly smaller,

found in eastern Canada, Minnesota, Wisconsin and
Michigan.

Age and Growth – Pups weigh ¾ to 1¼ pounds at
birth and grow to full size in 1 to 2 years. Males
measure 5 to 6½ feet from head to tip of tail and
weigh 90 to 130 pounds. Females weigh about 20
percent less. Gray wolves live up to 12 years.

Senses – Sense of smell, excellent; hearing, very
good; eyesight, fair. Wolves rely on scent and sound
when hunting and for detecting grizzlies, lynx and
wolverines, which prey on their pups.

Sign – Tracks (p. 121) are often seen on sandy or
muddy logging roads. Well-worn trails across frozen
lakes indicate wolf-pack crossings. Droppings
resemble those of large dogs, but contain bits of hair
and bone.

Social Interaction – Wolves live in packs of 5 to 25
animals. Each pack establishes a territory by scenting
the boundaries with urine and droppings. A dominant
male (the *alpha male*), his female partner (the *alpha
female*) and the next-highest-ranking male (the *beta
male*) make all decisions involving activities of the
pack, including when and where it hunts. All adults
in the pack care for the pups.

Howling gray wolf

Deep, drawn-out howls, initiated by the pack leaders, assemble the hunting pack and call in other pack members to share in the kill. Tail position indicates degree of dominance; the more dominant the wolf, the higher it holds its tail.

Breeding – The mating habits of the gray wolf are unique, with pairs commonly mating for life. In late winter, the alpha male and female frequently nuzzle each other in displays of affection. They breed about 2 weeks later. The beta male may also breed with the alpha female, but no other pack members take part in breeding. The pair digs a den in a hillside or riverbank, and a litter of 6 or 7 pups is delivered in spring.

Habitat – Found along the U.S.-Canada border and northward into the arctic islands, the gray wolf requires large expanses of land for hunting. It is found in vast forests and on mountain foothills and tundra, usually far from humans.

Food Habits – Wolf packs hunt from late afternoon through the night. On a single hunt, they may travel up to 50 miles in pursuit of deer, caribou or moose. They also hunt for rabbits, hares, beavers, squirrels, marmots, mice and, occasionally, livestock. After feeding, they usually rest in nearby cover until the next day's hunt.

Movement – Pack territories range in size from 100 to 600 square miles. Wolves that feed primarily on caribou may follow the migrating herds up to 500 miles. Wolves can run up to 40 mph, but they normally pursue their prey in a steady trot of about 5 mph. By maintaining that pace for up to 20 hours, they can tire most prey, making it more vulnerable to an attack.

Population – Declining in areas where forests are being cleared or problem wolves are being shot by ranchers. With their low reproductive rate and large territory requirements, wolves are not abundant anywhere.

Hunting Strategies – Because wolves roam so widely, most hunters use snowmobiles to locate and follow the pack. Hunters make the final stalk on foot to get within shooting range without being heard. In parts of Canada, an unused big-game tag allows you to take a wolf. Trappers account for many more wolves than hunters.

Trophy Records – No official record, but gray wolves have been known to reach 175 pounds.

Eating Quality – Poor; wolves are hunted for their valuable hide.

Coyote
(Canis latrans)

Common Names – Prairie wolf, brush wolf.

Description – Often mistaken for the gray wolf, the coyote is usually less than half as large with much shorter hair and a thinner muzzle. The upper body of both sexes varies from gray to yellowish or reddish brown, interspersed with black; the throat and undersides are white.

Age and Growth – At birth, pups weigh ¾ to 1¼ pounds. They are fully grown in about a year and live up to 12. Males measure 3½ to 4½ feet long and weigh 25 to 35 pounds. Females weigh about 20 percent less.

Senses – Sense of smell, excellent; eyesight and hearing, very good. Coyotes often locate prey by following a scent trail. In winter, they stand motionless and listen for mice moving beneath the snow.

Sign – Tracks (p. 121) look similar to those of domestic dogs. Droppings may contain bits of hair and are often found at intersections of game trails. Dens, which are usually dug into riverbanks or steep hillsides, often have trampled vegetation and the remains of prey nearby.

Social Interaction – Coyotes live in family groups consisting of a pair of adults and their young. The group establishes a territory by scenting dirt piles, stumps and brush with urine. At first, adults bring back small prey for the pups, but by early fall, the young coyotes and adults are hunting as a pack. By midwinter, the young disperse, relocating as much as 40 miles away.

Like gray wolves, coyotes howl to communicate each other's location within the territory. The pups make a high-pitched whine if separated from their parents.

Breeding – Coyotes mate in midwinter. After breeding, the male may leave the family territory to search for other females in heat. If he encounters a male of another family group, they may battle for breeding rights, with one pinning the other to the ground and

Coyote pups

biting it in the neck. In spring, a mating pair digs a den in which they can care for their litter of 5 or 6 pups. Once the pups begin to hunt with the adults, the den is abandoned.

Coyotes sometimes breed with domestic dogs to produce hybrids, or "coy-dogs," which look nearly identical to purebred coyotes.

Habitat – Found from Alaska to Mexico, coyotes are one of the most adaptable North American game animals. They prefer to hunt in rolling grasslands, and they use brush patches for cover.

Food Habits – Coyotes do most of their hunting after dark, but may hunt anytime. Their primary prey includes rabbits, hares and rodents, but the pack may hunt large animals, such as deer and even livestock. When pursuing a good-sized animal, they work as a relay team, with one or two chasing it in a large circle while the others rest. After making a kill and feeding, they bed nearby in heavy cover. Coyotes also feed on grasses, fruits, berries, domestic chickens and carrion.

Movement – Coyotes normally have a territory of 10 to 40 square miles. In mountainous areas, deep snow forces them down to the valleys in fall; in spring, they move back to the high country. Coyotes can sprint up to 35 mph, fast enough to overtake a deer.

Population – Increasing; with farming and logging creating an abundance of open areas and edge habitat, coyotes have expanded their range.

Hunting Strategies – The vast majority of coyotes are taken by hunters using predator calls, which imitate the scream of a wounded rabbit. Some hunters prefer to glass open areas and make long-range shots with varmint rifles.

Trophy Records – No official record, but coyotes up to 75 pounds have been reported.

Eating Quality – Poor; coyotes are shot for their pelts.

Red fox – red phase

Red Fox
(Vulpes vulpes)

Description – There are 4 color phases. The common red phase has a rusty coat with white undersides, chin and cheeks; the legs and top of the tail are black. Other phases include black; silver, the rarest; and *cross*, with a black band over the shoulders. All have white-tipped tails. The sexes look alike.

Age and Growth – The pups, which weigh 3 to 5 ounces at birth, grow to full size in about 8 months and live up to 12 years. Adult males measure 36 to 42 inches from head to tip of tail and weigh 8 to 12 pounds. Females are slightly smaller.

Senses – Sense of smell and hearing, excellent; eyesight, very good. Like coyotes, red fox locate most of their prey by smell. On a calm day, they can hear a mouse squeak at up to 100 yards.

Sign – A walking red fox leaves tracks (p. 121) in a straight line. The droppings usually contain bits of hair or feathers. The dens, which have a foot-wide opening with a pile of dirt on the downhill side, are dug into streambanks and hillsides.

Red fox – black phase   *Red fox – cross phase*

Red fox – silver phase

Red fox pouncing on mouse

Social Interaction – Red fox establish territories in the same manner as coyotes do, urinating on stumps and brush. Both parents care for the young, bringing them food and later teaching them to hunt. By the end of summer, the young can take care of themselves, so they disperse to set up their own territories, often traveling 40 miles or more.

Fairly vocal, red fox make short, yapping barks to locate each other and loud growls and hisses to intimidate intruders.

Breeding – In midwinter, males travel through females' territories, barking almost continuously to draw a response. If a female is interested, she answers with a high-pitched whine. Males fight for breeding rights by punching with the front feet, charging each other and biting. Once a male finds a mate, the two become nearly inseparable, traveling and hunting together until they breed in late winter. Then, both dig a den or they may take over a woodchuck burrow, where the litter of 4 to 8 pups is delivered in early spring.

Habitat – Found in a wide variety of habitats throughout the U.S. and Canada, the red fox prefers edge habitat, particularly where there is a patchwork of farm fields and wood lots. There, they can usually find an abundance of small prey. In heavily forested areas, they seek out clearings resulting from logging or fires.

Food Habits – Red fox usually hunt after dark and rest in thickets or under trees and rock ledges during the day. Their favorite food is mice, but they also feed on squirrels, rabbits, hares, ground-nesting birds, woodchucks and even domestic chickens. They jump high into the air to pounce on their prey (above), pin it to the ground with their front feet and kill it with a quick bite.

Movement – Because mice are so plentiful, the red fox can survive in a relatively small territory, usually less than 5 square miles. They can run even faster than coyotes, reaching speeds up to 45 mph.

Population – Stable throughout most of the range; increasing in areas where large forests are being partially logged.

Hunting Strategies – On a traditional southern fox hunt, hounds track the fox, while hunters follow on horseback. After the hounds pin down the fox, the hunters often choose to let it go. Fox can also be hunted like coyotes, using predator calls to draw them into shooting range.

Eating Quality – Poor; hunted for sport or pelts.

Gray Fox
(Urocyon cinereoargenteus)

Description – Similar in size to the red fox, but easily distinguished by the gray fur on the back, head and tail. The ears, sides of the head and flanks are rust-colored; the undersides, white. The sexes are identical in appearance.

Age and Growth – The pups, which weigh 3 to 5 ounces at birth, grow to full size in about 8 months. Adults measure 36 to 42 inches from head to tip of tail and weigh 7 to 13 pounds. Gray fox live up to 10 years.

Senses – Sense of smell, excellent; eyesight and hearing, very good.

Sign – Tracks (p. 121) of a walking gray fox, like those of a walking red fox, are laid down in a straight line. But the prints are smaller, resembling those of a domestic cat. The blackish droppings contain bits of hair, feathers or berries. The burrows look like those of a red fox, but are often in heavier cover.

Social Interaction – The social habits and vocalizations of the gray fox are very similar to those of the red fox, but their bark is raspier.

Breeding – Gray fox breed in late winter. In spring, a litter of 3 to 5 pups is delivered in a secluded den in a burrow, hollow log, stump or rock pile. Both parents feed and care for the pups until they are ready to hunt on their own.

Habitat – Found in the southern and eastern U.S. and throughout Mexico, the gray fox prefers the dense cover of swamps, grown-over clear-cuts and mesquite thickets.

Food Habits – Gray fox usually hunt after dark and rest in thick cover or in their den during the day. In cloudy weather, they may hunt anytime.

Common prey includes rabbits, hares, mice, snakes, insects, ground-nesting birds and carrion. Gray fox also feed heavily on berries, acorns and fruits, especially those of persimmon trees.

Movement – The gray fox is unique among canines in that it has strongly curved claws, which enable it to climb trees to escape predators and catch prey. Young fox may travel 50 miles to establish their own territory, which is usually less than 10 square miles. Considerably slower than red fox, grays can run up to 25 mph.

Population – Stable throughout most of their range.

Hunting Strategies – Most hunters sit in a ground blind and use a predator call to draw gray fox into shooting range. They can also be hunted with hounds, in the same manner as red fox.

Eating Quality – Poor; the gray fox is hunted for sport and the pelt.

72

White-phase and blue-phase (inset) arctic fox

Arctic Fox
(Alopex lagopus)

Description – Arctic fox, unlike other foxes, change color seasonally. In summer, both sexes are brownish gray, with yellowish white undersides, neck and flanks; in winter, white or bluish. White-phase fox are pure white, except for a black nose; blue-phase, bluish gray to bluish brown, sometimes with black head and feet. Both phases occur throughout the range, but one phase tends to be dominant in a particular region. Arctic fox are slightly smaller than red fox.

Age and Growth – At birth, arctic fox pups may weigh only 2 ounces, but they grow rapidly and reach full size by fall. Adults measure 28 to 36 inches from head to tip of tail and weigh 5 to 12 pounds. Males are slightly larger than females. Arctic fox live up to 10 years.

Senses – Hearing, eyesight and sense of smell, excellent. Arctic fox can sniff out lemmings and

Arctic fox in summer

voles burrowed beneath the snow, and smell carrion from a great distance.

Sign – The tracks (p.121) are commonly seen in the snow and along sandy riverbanks, lakeshores or coastlines. Droppings resemble those of the red fox. Dens, marked by dirt piles with lush grasses growing on them, are usually located on a south-facing bank or hillside and have multiple entrances. The lush growth around the dens is a result of fertilization by the foxes' droppings.

Social Interaction – Arctic fox live in family groups in spring and summer, but are solitary the rest of the year. Many animals may congregate, however, to feed on a carcass. The raspy bark alerts family members when another animal intrudes on their territory.

Breeding – Competing males scream and hiss at each other and wage fierce, sometimes bloody, fights for breeding rights; mating takes place in spring. The male and female dig a new den or move into an old one, and the litter, which averages 6 pups, is delivered in late spring or early summer. Males play an important role in parenting, bringing food to the den, guarding the pups against predators and staying with the young until they move out in early fall to establish their own territories.

Habitat – Arctic fox inhabit the northern reaches of Canada and Alaska, and their tracks have been spotted within a few hundred miles of the North Pole.

They're found on the tundra and along arctic shorelines, mainly in sandy areas where they can excavate dens above the permafrost. Arctic fox are capable of surviving the most severe climatic conditions, including temperatures down to -60°F.

Food Habits – Arctic fox hunt and feed at night or during low-light periods. In summer, they rely mainly on lemmings and other small rodents, birds, fish and sometimes carrion. They can usually find adequate food near their den site. In winter, they may have to travel hundreds of miles to find food, and they depend more heavily on carrion, such as leftovers of caribou killed by timber wolves. They also venture far out on the polar ice cap to feed on seals killed by polar bears. Sometimes they become stranded on an ice floe and drift for days before reaching land.

Movement – The size of an arctic fox's territory depends on food availability. The size expands as winter approaches and food becomes harder to find.

Population – Cyclical; the fox population increases following a high lemming year and decreases after a low one.

Hunting Strategies – Some arctic fox are taken by caribou hunters or coastal duck hunters, but trappers account for the largest harvest.

Eating Quality – Poor; arctic fox are hunted mainly for their valuable pelt.

Raccoon
(Procyon lotor)

Common Names – Coon, ringtail.

Description – The raccoon is the only ring-tailed animal with a black face mask. The body of both sexes is a grizzled grayish brown above and grayish below. Coon in the northern part of the range have a darker back than their southern counterparts. In coastal regions, they have an overall reddish tinge.

Age and Growth – Weighing 2 to 3 ounces at birth, coon grow continuously through life, with males reaching a length of 32 to 42 inches from head to tip of tail and a weight of 15 to 30 pounds, and occasionally, 40. Females weigh about 15 percent less than males. Coon live up to 5 years.

Senses – Hearing and sense of touch, excellent; eyesight and night vision, good; sense of smell, fair. Coon use their forepaws, which are very sensitive and nimble, for finding, catching and eating food. They rank among the most intelligent of all game animals.

Sign – Tracks (p. 121) and feeding sign, such as crayfish parts and clamshells, are commonly seen along lakeshores and streambanks. Coon leave long, granular droppings on certain rocks, logs and stumps near feeding areas. They usually build dens in hollow trees, and sometimes in old woodchuck burrows, in tall grass or beneath tree roots. They line the dens with dried leaves.

Social Interaction – Adults are solitary, but during a severe winter storm, many huddle together in the same den for several days.

When cornered, coon snarl, growl or hiss. "Churring" means the animal is content. Females make a low-pitched "purr" to call their young.

Breeding – Coon mate from late winter into spring. Females breed only once, but males mate with several females. A litter of 2 to 6 young, is delivered in late spring to early summer. If a female loses her litter early in the season, she may attempt to mate again.

Habitat – Found throughout North America, with the exception of Alaska, much of northern Canada and parts of the Rocky Mountain states. Coon prefer forested areas near lakes and streams, but also inhabit farmland with scattered wood lots.

Food Habits – Raccoon are night feeders, seldom coming out to feed during the day. They may travel several miles on their nightly feeding run.

Coon are omnivorous, eating everything from fruits to fish. Some of their favorite foods include persimmon fruits, grapes, plums, nuts and corn; they also eat crayfish, insects, frogs and clams. In the northern part of their range, coon put on a heavy fat layer in fall to help get them through the winter.

Movement – Raccoon spend most of their time in an area of 3 to 5 square miles, ranging more widely only when food is scarce. During their first fall, young coon abandon their mother's territory to establish a territory of their own. Excellent climbers, coon scurry up trees to escape danger. They do not hibernate in winter, but animals in the northern part of the range lie dormant in their dens for extended periods, especially in bitterly cold weather.

Population – Increasing; with the lower demand for fur, fewer coons are being killed for their pelts.

Hunting Strategies – The most effective method is hunting at night with coonhounds. The dogs course widely to find fresh scent, and then the chase begins. The dogs yowl loudly as they trail the coon and begin baying once it is treed. This signals the hunters, who then use headlamps to spot the coon and small caliber rifles to dispatch it.

Eating Quality – Good, although coon are hunted mostly for their pelt. The meat, which tastes much like lamb, is somewhat oily, and large males may taste quite gamey. Removing all fat before cooking improves the flavor.

Rabbits & Hares

Order Lagomorpha

Favorites among small game hunters, rabbits and hares are small grazing animals with large ears, long hind legs and short tails. Their chisellike upper incisors, like those of rodents, grow continuously and are worn down by gnawing. But rodents have upper and lower incisors; rabbits and hares, only uppers.

Although the names rabbit and hare are often used interchangeably, this is a mistake. Rabbits are born naked and helpless, with their eyes shut, in fur-lined nests; they weigh only about 1 ounce. Hares,

including jackrabbits, may weigh up to 6 ounces at birth; they have fur, their eyes are open and they can run shortly after they're born.

Hares are generally larger than rabbits, with bigger ears and longer, more powerful, hind legs. Their habitat is usually more open, and they evade predators by outrunning them, rather than hiding in dense cover or ducking into burrows.

Both rabbits and hares are highly prolific, commonly producing several litters each year. The young usually reach full size within a few months.

Rabbit and hare populations undergo dramatic cycles (p. 91), with numbers in good years often ten times as high as those in poor years. Populations of predators that rely on rabbits and hares for food experience corresponding, but less dramatic, cycles.

Eastern Cottontail

(Sylvilagus floridanus)

Common Name – Cottontail.

Description – Named for its fluffy, white tail, the cottontail has grayish to reddish brown fur with black tips. The undersides are white and the nape of the neck, rust colored. The coat is a lighter color in winter than in summer. A cottontail has ears from 1¾ to 2¾ inches long.

Age and Growth – Eastern cottontails measure 14 to 19 inches in length and weigh 2½ to 3½ pounds.

In captivity, cottontails may live 10 years; in the wild, 2 or 3. More than 80 percent of them are killed by predators or hunters or die of natural causes each year.

Senses – Hearing, excellent; eyesight and sense of smell, good. Cottontails normally detect predators by sound or sight and use their sense of smell to find food, even when it is covered by snow. Because their eyes are on the side of the head, cottontails can remain motionless, yet have a 360-degree field of vision.

Sign – Tracks (p. 122) are seldom visible, except in soft snow. Cottontails make trails, or *runways*, in tall grass and use them as escape routes. The pea-sized droppings are dark brown. Feeding sign includes cleanly clipped twigs and stripped-off bark on young trees.

Social Interaction – Cottontails are solitary, even though males will tolerate other rabbits living nearby. Females establish territories, which they defend against other females.

Like other rabbits, cottontails thump their hind feet, making vibrations that signal danger. Females may purr when nursing and males sometimes growl to assert dominance.

Breeding – Cottontails breed over a 3- to 6-month period, beginning in early spring. They usually have 4 litters each year, but have been known to produce as many as 8.

Before breeding, males box, kick or bite to determine social rank. A dominant male selects a female, and a courtship ritual ensues in which they chase, charge and jump over each other. The female eventually accepts his advances, but she quickly runs him off after breeding is completed. He then moves on to breed other females.

The female digs a 4-inch-deep depression in the ground and lines it with a mixture of belly fur and grass. She covers the litter, which consists of 3 to 6 young, with a blanket made of the same materials. She guards the nest closely, and chases off predators that venture too close. Within hours of giving birth, she is ready to breed again.

Cottontail litter

Habitat – Cottontails are highly adaptable, living just about anywhere, with the exception of extensive forests. They're most common in thickets and brush piles in small woodlands and along forest edges and hedgerows.

Hawk taking cottontail

Food Habits – Cottontails feed in early morning and late afternoon. They spend the middle of the day resting in a *form*, a shallow depression in the grass or snow. But strong winds, rain or snow may drive them out of their form into heavier cover.

Common summertime foods include grasses, forbs, fruits and berries, and small grains, especially wheat and soybeans. In winter, they feed primarily on twigs and bark of young trees and shrubs.

Movement – Cottontails do not travel great distances, normally spending their entire life in an area of less than 10 acres. But they become intimately familiar with that territory and refuse to leave it when threatened. To escape, they usually run in a large circle, returning to their starting point. They run at speeds up to 20 mph.

Population – With no predation, a pair of cottontails could multiply to 350,000 in 5 years. This tremendous reproductive rate explains why hunters can take 30 million each year without harming the population.

Hunting Strategies – The most productive method for hunting cottontails is to flush them from heavy cover using beagles or basset hounds. These slow-moving dogs keep the rabbits moving but won't push them so hard that they scamper into another animal's burrow. If you wait at the spot where you jumped the rabbit, it will usually circle back, offering you a shot.

If you don't have a dog, walk through thin strips of cover, such as a brushy fenceline. In broader expanses of cover, a cottontail will hold tight in its form and allow you to walk by.

A flushed rabbit runs erratically, so most hunters use shotguns with fairly open chokes.

Eating Quality – Excellent; the light-colored meat has a fine texture and tastes much like chicken.

Brush Rabbit

(Sylvilagus bachmani)

Description – The brush rabbit is similar to the eastern cottontail, but the coat is slightly browner and the tail has much less white. The coat turns lighter colored in winter. The ears measure $1\frac{1}{2}$ to $2\frac{1}{2}$ inches long.

Age and Growth – Smaller than eastern cottontails, brush rabbits measure 11 to 15 inches in length and weigh only 1 to 2 pounds. They live up to 3 years.

Sign – Tracks (p. 122) are similar in shape to those of the eastern cottontail, but smaller. The trails, droppings and feeding sign are identical.

Social Interaction – Brush rabbits are loners most of the year, although several of them may feed in the same area. A rabbit that approaches too close to another one, however, risks being chased off. Brush rabbits communicate in much the same way as eastern cottontails.

Breeding – The brush rabbit's breeding habits are identical to those of eastern cottontails, but litters are slightly smaller.

Habitat – Found in forests along the Pacific Coast, brush rabbits prefer clear-cuts that have grown back to heavy brush, thorny shrubs and evergreen oak thickets.

Food Habits – More secretive than eastern cottontails, brush rabbits do most of their feeding after dark and spend midday resting in their forms. If the cover is heavy enough, they may feed early and late in the day.

In summer, the diet includes green clover, berries, roots and various grasses. In winter, they browse on shrubs, such as salal, and other woody vegetation, like young Douglas fir.

Movement – Brush rabbits spend their entire life within a few acres and do not move seasonally.

Population – Stable throughout most of the range.

Hunting Strategies – Because of their small size, brush rabbits are not hunted as heavily as most other rabbits, but you can use the same techniques as you would for eastern cottontails.

Eating Quality – Excellent; the meat is indistinguishable from that of eastern cottontail.

Mountain Cottontail
(Sylvilagus nuttallii)

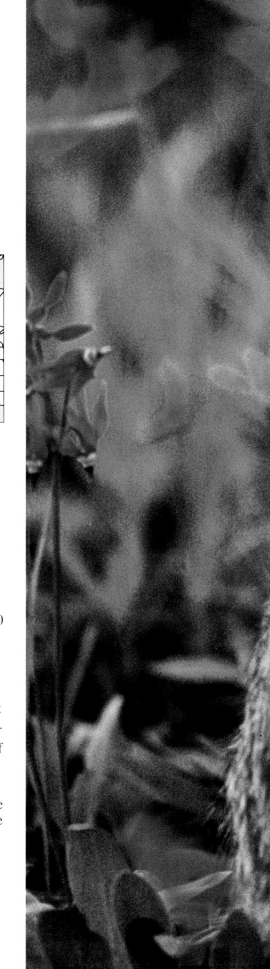

Common Names – Nuttall's cottontail, western cottontail.

Description – Mountain cottontails are grayish to yellowish brown with white undersides and tail. Their rounded, black-tipped ears measure slightly over 2 inches in length.

Age and Growth – Mountain cottontails measure 13½ to 15½ inches in length and weigh 1½ to 3 pounds. They live up to 4 years.

Senses – Hearing, excellent; sense of smell and eyesight, good.

Sign – Tracks, trails, droppings and feeding sign are similar to those of eastern cottontails.

Social Interaction – Mountain cottontails are solitary, except when they congregate in feeding areas. They communicate in much the same way as eastern cottontails.

Breeding – Prior to breeding, males determine dominance in the same manner as eastern cottontails. Mating takes place from late winter to mid-summer, and a female bears 2 to 5 litters, each with 3 to 8 young.

Habitat – Found in western mountains and foothills at elevations of 6,000 to 11,000 feet, mountain cottontails inhabit brushy stream corridors and rocky slopes covered with sagebrush.

Food Habits – Mountain cottontails feed from sunset to a few hours after sunrise, spending the rest of the day in their forms. Sagebrush makes up most of their diet, but they prefer green grasses, when available. They also eat twigs and needles of junipers, sometimes climbing 8 feet up a tree to feed.

Movement – Mountain cottontails spend their entire life on a few acres of ground. When alarmed, they retreat into rock crevices or the burrows of prairie dogs and ground squirrels.

Population – Stable overall, although individual populations may fluctuate greatly because of predation, disease and weather. But the high reproductive rate means numbers can rebound quickly.

Hunting Strategies – Still-hunting is the best method. Hunting with dogs does not work as well as it does for eastern cottontails; mountain cottontails will usually scamper down a burrow if a dog is in pursuit.

Eating Quality – Excellent; the meat is indistinguishable from that of the eastern cottontail.

Desert Cottontail

(Sylvilagus audubonii)

Common Names – Audubon cottontail, prairie dog rabbit.

Description – Desert cottontails are easily identified by their yellowish brown body, bright rust-colored legs, feet and nape and disproportionately large ears, which measure $2\frac{3}{4}$ to $3\frac{1}{2}$ inches long. The tail and undersides are white.

Age and Growth – Desert cottontails measure 12 to $16\frac{1}{2}$ inches in length and weigh $1\frac{1}{2}$ to $2\frac{3}{4}$ pounds. They live up to 4 years.

Senses – Hearing, excellent; sense of smell and eyesight, good. Their large ears gather sound, accounting for their superb hearing.

Sign – Tracks (p. 122), trails, droppings and feeding sign are nearly identical to those of eastern cottontails. The droppings are often found on logs, which desert cottontails use as lookout posts.

Social Interaction – Desert cottontails are solitary, but not territorial. They communicate in the same manner as eastern cottontails.

Breeding – The mating ritual is much like that of the eastern cottontail, but the desert cottontail breeds year-round and produces 2 to 5 litters, each with 1 to 6 young.

Habitat – Inhabiting foothills, valleys, open plains, grasslands and deserts of the arid Southwest, desert cottontails commonly use sagebrush, creosote bush and scattered junipers as cover.

Food Habits – They do most of their feeding from late afternoon to well after dark, but desert cottontails may feed anytime of the day or night. When not feeding, they usually rest in another animal's burrow. Their diet includes grasses, mesquite, cactus and the bark and twigs of woody plants.

Movement – Desert cottontails spend their life in an area of 15 acres or less. They escape predators by climbing up sloping trees, hiding in thickets or ducking into burrows of other animals.

Population – Generally stable, but cyclical.

Hunting Strategies – Still-hunt edges of brushy cover and try to spot a rabbit before it flushes. Even if it does flush, it will usually stop after running a short distance, offering you an easy shot. Like mountain cottontails, they quickly hide in burrows if pursued by dogs.

Eating Quality – Excellent; the meat tastes identical to that of the eastern cottontail.

Swamp Rabbit

(Sylvilagus aquaticus)

Common Name – Cane-cutter.

Description – Largest of the North American rabbits, the swamp rabbit has yellowish brown fur with black tips, and buff-gray or white undersides. It has a cinnamon ring around each eye, 2½-inch ears and a relatively thin tail.

Age and Growth – Swamp rabbits measure 16 to 22 inches in length and weigh 2½ to 6 pounds. They live up to 3 years.

Senses – Hearing, excellent; eyesight and sense of smell, good.

Sign – Tracks, trails, droppings and feeding sign resemble those of eastern cottontails and are usually near water. The nest is a pile of sticks lined with grass.

Social Interaction – Swamp rabbits are solitary and territorial. To establish a territory, they scent brush and stumps by rubbing them with a gland under their chin. They screech to warn others of predators.

Breeding – Males compete for breeding rights in the same way as eastern cottontails. Mating takes place from midwinter to early fall, with the dominant male breeding most females that are in heat. They produce up to 5 litters a year, each with 2 or 3 young.

Habitat – The species name, *aquaticus*, refers to this rabbit's affinity for water. It inhabits cypress swamps, bottomlands, marshes and banks of rivers and drainage ditches in the south-central U.S.

Food Habits – Swamp rabbits feed around sunrise and sunset, spending midday in forms or holes in rotten trees. In summer, they feed mainly on aquatic plants, such as cane, explaining the name "cane-cutter." Other summertime foods include corn and grasses. In winter, they eat twigs and bark of woody plants.

Movement – A swamp rabbit's territory is usually 10 acres or less. When chased by a predator, it dives and resurfaces beneath roots or overhanging trees.

Population – Declining in many areas due to loss of marsh habitat.

Hunting Strategies – Popular game animals because of their large size, swamp rabbits are hunted with the same techniques used for eastern cottontails.

Eating Quality – Excellent; much like eastern cottontail.

Marsh Rabbit

(Sylvilagus palustris)

Description – Noticeably smaller than the swamp rabbit, the marsh rabbit has dark brown fur with black tips and a cinnamon-colored nape. The undersides are light brown to buff; the tail, brownish or grayish. The ears are short, measuring only 1½ to 2 inches.

Age and Growth – Marsh rabbits reach 14 to 18 inches in length and 2½ to 4 pounds in weight. Their longevity is unknown, but is probably no more than 3 years.

Senses – Hearing, excellent; eyesight, very good; sense of smell, good.

Sign – The trails, droppings, feeding sign and tracks are similar to those of eastern cottontails. But marsh rabbits sometimes walk on their hind legs only, so the track pattern may lack the front footprints found in the tracks of other rabbits and hares.

Social Interaction – The social habits of the marsh rabbit are poorly known. Like the swamp rabbit, it has a scent gland under the chin, leading some biologists to believe it is territorial.

Breeding – Marsh rabbits mate year-round, producing up to 6 litters, each with 2 to 5 young.

Habitat – Never far from water, marsh rabbits inhabit bottomlands, swamps, lakeshores and coastal waterways of the southeastern U.S.

Food Habits – Highly secretive, marsh rabbits normally feed after dark, spending the day resting in forms. Their summertime diet includes grasses, roots and marsh vegetation, such as cane stems. In winter, they eat leaves and twigs of deciduous trees.

Movement – Even more water-oriented than swamp rabbits, marsh rabbits often swim across a pond rather than hop around it. They sometimes escape predators by floating with only their eyes and nose above the surface.

Population – Declining in areas where marshes are being drained.

Hunting Strategies – One of the most effective techniques is hunting islands in lakes or swamps. Drivers use beagles to flush rabbits out of the brush and push them toward posters.

Eating Quality – Excellent; as good as eastern cottontail.

Snowshoe Hare

(Lepus americanus)

Common Names – Varying hare, snowshoe rabbit, snowshoe.

Description – Snowshoe hares are named for their huge hind feet, which enable them to bound across deep, fresh snow. In summer, their coat and tail are brown or brownish gray; in fall and spring, a brown-and-white mixture; in winter, all white. The undersides are whitish all year. Snowshoes have 2½- to 3¼-inch, black-tipped ears.

Age and Growth – Smallest of the hares, snowshoes measure 16 to 21 inches long and weigh 3 to 4 pounds. They live up to 5 years.

Senses – Hearing, very good; eyesight, good; sense of smell, fair.

Sign – Tracks (p.122) are usually found in snow. Summer trails zigzag through thick vegetation; winter trails in snow may be a foot deep. Droppings are round and dark brown. Tree trunks stripped of bark show where snowshoes have been feeding.

Social Interaction – Snowshoe hares are solitary, but, when populations are high, they may feed in small groups.

Snowshoes thump their feet loudly to alert others of danger. Females grunt softly to call their young, and males make a raspy growl when fighting.

Breeding – From late winter to midsummer, males fight for breeding rights by violently slashing each other with their sharp hind claws, occasionally causing serious injury or death. Prolific breeders, snowshoes produce 2 to 5 litters, each with 2 to 6 young, annually.

Snowshoe in winter and summer (inset) coat

Habitat – Found throughout most of the northern half of North America, snowshoes prefer large forested areas with plenty of swamps, brushy lakeshores and streambanks, and dense thickets resulting from clear-cuts.

Food Habits – Snowshoes do most of their feeding after dark, spending the day bedding in forms in the grass or snow. But they may feed early or late in the day in cloudy weather.

A snowshoe's summertime diet includes most any type of green vegetation and buds of trees and shrubs. In fall, it browses on twigs of birch, aspen, poplar, willow, maple and alder trees. Winter foods include conifer needles and the bark of alder and aspen trees.

Movement – Snowshoes normally spend their lives in an area of 10 to 100 acres. But when populations are high, they have to cover more ground, sometimes several square miles, to find adequate food.

To evade predators, snowshoes sprint away at speeds up to 30 mph. Their ability to change direction instantly makes it difficult for predators to catch them and for hunters to make running shots.

Population – Numbers cycle about every 10 years between extreme highs and lows (chart below). When snowshoe hares overpopulate their habitat, food shortages, disease and stress cause the population to crash.

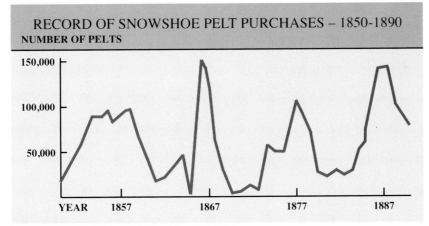

RECORD OF SNOWSHOE PELT PURCHASES – 1850-1890
NUMBER OF PELTS

150,000
100,000
50,000

YEAR   1857   1867   1877   1887

SNOWSHOE POPULATIONS peak about every 10 years, as shown by the Hudson's Bay Company pelt-purchase records over a 40-year period.

Hunting Strategies – The most widely used method is hunting with a beagle or other small, slow-working dog to flush snowshoes from dense, low-growing thickets.

Wait near the spot the dog first detected scent, because snowshoes usually circle back to the spot from which they flushed.

Still-hunting works best in winter; watch for a snowshoe's black eyes and black-tipped ears against the snow. Still-hunting is even more effective if the snow melts in midwinter, because you can easily see the white animals against the brown background.

Eating Quality – Good; the meat tends to be drier, tougher and gamier tasting than rabbit, so many hunters use it in stews.

Black-Tailed Jackrabbit

(Lepus californicus)

Common Name – Blacktail jack.

Description – Easily identified by their black-topped tail, black rump patch and 7-inch black-tipped ears, blacktail jacks have brownish gray fur with black tips on the upper body; grayish white fur on the chin and undersides. Unlike snowshoes, they do not change color seasonally.

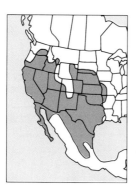

Age and Growth – Blacktail jacks measure 18 to 24 inches long and weigh 3 to 7½ pounds. They live up to 8 years.

Senses – Hearing, excellent; sense of smell, very good; eyesight, good.

Sign – Tracks (p. 122) are similar in shape to those of snowshoe hares, but smaller. Well-worn trails link feeding and resting sites. Droppings are round and dark brown. Forms measuring about 16 inches long, 5 inches wide and 3 inches deep are scratched into the ground, usually under bushes.

Social Interaction – Blacktail jacks often feed in small groups. Pregnant females establish small territories in which they raise their young. Females make a high-pitched squeal to assemble the young, and males emit a soft growl when fighting. Adults flash the white underside of the tail when fleeing, to alert others to danger.

Breeding – Males compete for breeding rights by boxing or biting, much like snowshoes. Blacktail jacks breed from early winter to early fall, producing up to 4 litters, each with 2 to 4 young. The female places each newborn in a separate form, making it difficult for predators to wipe out the entire litter.

Habitat – Found in the southwestern U.S. and Mexico, blacktail jacks inhabit sparsely vegetated deserts, open prairies, mountain meadows, woodland edges and cultivated fields.

Food Habits – Primarily night feeders, blacktail jacks begin feeding in late afternoon and may continue until early morning. In midday, they take cover in forms beneath bushes or in clumps of grass.

The diet includes mesquite seeds, prickly pear cactus, sagebrush, greasewood, alfalfa and green grass.

Movement – Blacktail jacks spend their life within 1 or 2 square miles. When chased by a predator, they make periodic high leaps to keep track of their pursuer and get a better view of their escape route.

Population – Stable in the long term; populations of blacktail jacks, like those of snowshoe hares, undergo a 10-year cycle.

Hunting Strategies – Walk through bushes or tall grass to flush blacktail jacks from their forms into the open. Use a shotgun with an open choke, because jacks can sprint up to 35 mph.

Eating Quality – Poor; the meat is dryer and tougher than that of other hares.

Whitetail jack in summer and winter (inset) coat

White-Tailed Jackrabbit

(Lepus townsendii)

Common Name –
Whitetail jack.

Description – The brownish
gray summer coat is similar to
that of the blacktail jack, but
the top of the tail is white; the
black-tipped ears are shorter,
only 4 to 6 inches; and the
undersides are light tan.
Unlike blacktails, whitetails
in the North turn completely
white in winter, except for the black tips on the ears;
those in the South become pale brown.

Age and Growth – One of the largest North
American hares, the whitetail jack measures 22 to 26
inches long and weighs 6 to 10 pounds. It lives up to
6 years.

Senses – Hearing, excellent; sense of smell, very
good; eyesight, good.

Sign – Tracks, trails, forms, droppings and feeding
sign are similar to those of snowshoe hares.

Social Interaction – The social behavior of whitetail
jacks is much like that of snowshoes.

Breeding – Like other male hares, male whitetails
box and slash viciously for breeding rights. Mating
takes place from late winter to midsummer. But after
the dominant male has bred a particular female, she
may accept other males. Whitetail jacks produce up
to 4 litters a year, each with 3 or 4 young.

Habitat – Found in the west-central U.S., whitetail
jacks frequent pastures, prairies, grasslands and forest openings on mountain slopes. They take shelter
from winter storms in heavily wooded areas.

Food Habits – Very secretive, whitetail jacks feed
after dark and spend the day in their forms, which
are usually in tall grass or under bushes. In summer,
the diet includes alfalfa, clover, grass, vegetable
greens and weeds, particularly snakeweed; in winter,
shrubby vegetation, such as rabbitbrush.

Movement – Whitetail jacks spend most of their
life on a few square miles of ground, but they range
much more widely if food or water become scarce.
Exceptionally fast, they have been clocked at speeds
up to 45 mph.

Population – Stable; the population is increasing in
some areas, as development converts forested land
to a patchwork of wood lots and open areas, and
decreasing in others, as grassland is lost to intensive
farming.

Hunting Strategies – Use the same techniques as
you would for blacktail jacks, or glass the animals as
they rest beneath bushes, and take long shots with a
varmint rifle.

Eating Quality – Good; the meat is similar to that
of snowshoe hare.

94

Arctic hare in winter and summer (inset) coat

Arctic Hare

(Lepus arcticus)

Common Name – Polar hare.

Description – Like snowshoes, arctic hares are brownish in summer, white in winter and a brown-and-white mixture in

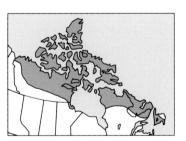

between. But arctic hares differ from snowshoes in that their tail stays white year-round. Their black-tipped ears are 2¾ to 3¼ inches long.

Age and Growth – Largest of the North American hares, the arctic hare measures 19 to 27 inches long and weighs 7 to 15 pounds. It lives up to 6 years.

Senses – Sense of smell, excellent; hearing, good; eyesight, fair.

Sign – Snow dens with 4-inch-wide openings and hard-packed trails reveal the arctic hares' winter location. Tracks and droppings are similar to those of snowshoe hares. Cleanly snipped willow shoots show where the animals have been browsing.

Social Interaction – In the southern part of their range, arctic hares are solitary or may form small groups. But in the northern part, feeding herds may number in the hundreds. In extremely cold weather, a few animals sometimes huddle together in forms to conserve body heat. Arctic hares communicate in much the same way as snowshoe hares.

Breeding – Like most other male hares, male arctics box for breeding rights. Mating takes place in late spring. The litter, delivered in early summer, numbers 4 to 8. Because of the short summer, it is unusual for arctic hares to have a second litter.

Habitat – Found on the tundra of northern Canada, the arctic islands and Greenland, arctic hares have the northernmost range of any North American hare.

Food Habits – Arctic hares feed during low-light periods, which, in summer, means from late afternoon to early morning. They spend midday sunning themselves on boulders. In winter, they may feed or rest most anytime.

Favorite summertime foods include grasses, sedges, berries and moss. In winter, they dig through crusted snow to find twigs and roots of shrubs, particularly dwarf willow. They also eat carrion.

Movement – Arctic hares spend their entire lives on a few hundred acres. They can run up to 30 mph.

Population – Stable, although numbers fluctuate greatly from year to year.

Hunting Strategies – Hunted mainly by Eskimos and Indians, using snares or traps.

Eating Quality – Fair; the white meat is extremely dry and tastes best if some fat is added.

New England Cottontail
(Sylvilagus transitionalis)

New England cottontails are nearly identical to eastern cottontails, except for their black-rimmed ears, black patch of fur on top of the head and slightly smaller size. Their feeding and mating habits are also similar, and they're hunted using the same methods.

Found in large, dense woodlands of the Northeast, New England cottontails prefer forests with plenty of underbrush resulting from fires or clear-cutting.

Populations of New England cottontails are steadily declining as forests mature and the understory disappears. Another problem is loss of large woodlands to housing, roads and industrial development.

Pygmy Rabbit
(Brachylagus idahoensis)

The smallest rabbit in North America, the pygmy rabbit weighs $1/2$ to 1 pound and measures 8 to 11 inches long. It has a brownish gray coat, sometimes with a pinkish tinge, and a gray tail. The undersides are tan.

Pygmy rabbits bear many similarities to mountain rabbits. They prefer the same type of habitat, eat the same foods and have similar breeding habits.

Unlike other rabbits, pygmies dig shallow, underground burrows, which have three or more entrances. When threatened, they often take shelter in these burrows, making them difficult to hunt.

European Hare

(Lepus europaeus)

Among the largest North American hares, European hares weigh 7 to 10 pounds and measure 25 to 28 inches long. The coat changes from brown with black tips in summer to gray in winter. The undersides are white.

Sometimes called "cape hares" or "brown hares," European hares were introduced into North America in 1893. They inhabit meadows, cultivated fields, rolling hills and small wood lots of the Great Lakes region.

Similar to snowhoe hares in food and breeding habits, European hares are generally hunted using the same techniques.

Antelope Jackrabbit

(Lepus alleni)

Named for their leaping ability, antelope jackrabbits are also known as Allen's or Mexican jackrabbits.

These large, long-eared hares weigh 6 to 12 pounds and measure 21 to 26 inches long. They have a grayish brown coat and white undersides.

Found in deserts and dry valleys of Arizona and Mexico, antelope jackrabbits eat mesquite, prickly pear cactus and a variety of grasses. Their breeding habits are similar to those of blacktail jacks.

Antelope jacks are hunted much the same way as other hares, but they can run up to 45 mph, presenting a greater shooting challenge.

Rodents
Order Rodentia

The name *Rodentia* comes from the Latin word *rodens,* meaning "gnawing," and refers to the animals' specialized incisors. The upper set works against the lower, keeping them both sharp for clipping vegetation.

Because their incisors grow continuously, rodents must gnaw enough to keep them worn down. If they don't, the teeth grow so long that the animal can't eat.

Rodents, which include such game animals as squirrels, chucks, prairie dogs and marmots, are the largest order of mammals, in terms of both number of species and number of individuals. The order also includes many animals of interest to trappers, such as beaver and muskrat, and numerous others, like gophers, rats and mice, viewed mainly as pests. Although short-lived, most of these animals are superabundant, because of their unmatched reproductive rates.

Squirrels are perhaps the most popular small-game animal; chucks, prairie dogs and marmots are pursued mainly by varmint hunters.

Most rodents stay active all year, but some hibernate in winter, surviving on stored fat reserves. Their body temperature may drop into the low 40s, so their metabolism is greatly reduced.

Hoary marmot

98

Eastern Gray Squirrel

(Sciurus carolinensis)

Common Names – Gray squirrel, cat squirrel, black squirrel, bushy tail.

Description – Most common of all North American tree squirrels, gray squirrels have a grayish body with whitish undersides. The bushy tail has white-tipped hairs. Both black and albino color phases are found throughout the range, often in discrete colonies.

Age and Growth – Gray squirrels measure 14 to 21 inches from head to tip of tail and weigh ¾ to 1¼ pounds. They live up to 6 years.

Senses – Eyesight, excellent; hearing and sense of smell, very good. Gray squirrels are experts at judging distance when jumping through treetops and quick to spot movement. They can easily find nuts buried a few inches below ground.

Sign – Gray squirrels build leafy nests in crotches of trees or weave them into branches, usually 25 feet or more off the ground. They also make dens in hollow trees. Their tracks (p. 123) resemble those of cottontail rabbits, but the front prints are not staggered as much. Cracked nutshells on the ground mark their favorite feeding spots.

Social Interaction – Grays do not defend territories, but are generally intolerant of other squirrels. In extremely cold weather, however, they may share nests.

Quite vocal, they may grunt, purr, bark or chatter their teeth when angry or nervous. Or, they may rapidly flick their tail.

Breeding – Gray squirrels mate twice a year – in late winter and again in early summer. Up to 5 males chase a female on the ground and through the trees, attempting to breed her; the most dominant male usually succeeds. Males may mate with several females. The young are born in early spring and late summer, with each litter numbering from 3 to 6.

Habitat – Found in mixed hardwood forests in the eastern half of the U. S. and parts of southern Canada, grays prefer forests that have dense undergrowth with some grassy openings and an abundance of mature oaks and other nut-producing trees. They also thrive in urban areas, especially parks.

Food Habits – Gray squirrels feed for 2 to 3 hours in early morning and again in late afternoon. They spend the middle of the day in their den or nest. They "scatter-hoard" their food in fall, burying individual nuts over a large area and digging them up again in winter and spring.

Important foods include acorns and other nuts, berries and corn. They occasionally eat insects, mushrooms and bird eggs.

Movement – Gray squirrels spend the majority of their time on only a few acres of ground, but they sometimes abandon this area in fall and relocate if the annual nut crop is poor. They have been known to make mass movements from one area to another to find food, with many perishing as they attempt to cross rivers and lakes.

Population – Fluctuates with the annual nut crop; a high population follows a year of good nut production, and vice versa.

Hunting Strategies – Look for woods with the most nests, and then stand or sit against a tree or stump to break up your outline. Remain motionless and wait for the squirrels to begin moving about. Still-hunting through the woods and searching with binoculars is also a proven method.

Eating Quality – Very good; the light-colored meat is usually mild and tender.

Typical gray squirrel nest

Eastern gray squirrel in gray, albino (left inset) and black (right inset) color phases

101

Fox Squirrel

(Sciurus niger)

Common Name – Mistakenly called red squirrels by some hunters.

Description – There are 3 color phases. The common fox squirrel gets its name from the orange color on the undersides, ear tips and top of the tail. The back and sides are a grizzled gray, sometimes with an orange tinge. Other phases include pure black and bright rust, which has brighter orange undersides than the common fox squirrel. The bright rust phase is most common in the western part of their range.

Age and Growth – Largest of all North American tree squirrels, fox squirrels measure 19 to 29 inches from head to tip of tail and weigh 1 to $2\frac{3}{4}$ pounds. They live up to 5 years.

Senses – Eyesight, excellent; senses of hearing and smell, very good. Fox squirrels are quick to spot movement and always watching for danger. Their sense of smell is important in locating buried nuts.

Sign – Nests are similar to those of gray squirrels, and at least 20 feet off the ground. Dens, made by gnawing holes in trees, are at least 10 feet off the ground and have 4-inch entrance holes. Nutshells found on stumps and logs identify favorite feeding spots. Tracks (p. 123) are identical to those of gray squirrels.

Social Interaction – Solitary animals, fox squirrels flick their tail and chatter their teeth to warn others encroaching on their feeding area. They may chase off an intruder, but usually avoid a fight. A squirrel that detects danger alerts other squirrels in the vicinity with a rapid series of "cherks." A relaxed squirrel sometimes makes a low-pitched chuckle.

Breeding – Breeding habits are nearly identical to those of gray squirrels, but males are more aggressive when establishing dominance, often biting and clawing each other. Litters, which include 2 to 4 young, are smaller than those of gray squirrels.

Habitat – Fox squirrels are found throughout the eastern U.S. and parts of southern Canada; they prefer farm groves, wood lots, timber strips and forest edges, as opposed to continuous forest.

Food Habits – Fox squirrels are most active in midday, often straying far from their dens in search of food. They seldom feed in the morning. Like gray squirrels, they scatter-hoard their food for winter.

Favorite foods are almost identical to those of gray squirrels, but fox squirrels eat more cultivated grains, because many live near agricultural areas.

Movement – Fox squirrels spend their entire life in an area of no more than 15 acres, unless forced to move by drought or crop failure. They spend more time on the ground than other tree squirrels. During cold or stormy weather, they usually stay within 15 yards of their den.

Population – Stable; the cutting of large forests has created an abundance of edge habitat and small wood lots.

Hunting Strategies – Similar to those used for gray squirrels, but best locations are often small wood lots around agricultural fields.

Eating Quality – Very good; the meat tastes much like that of the gray squirrel. Old fox squirrels are considerably tougher than young ones.

Common fox squirrel

Fox squirrel – bright rust phase

Fox squirrel – black phase

Red Squirrel
(Tamiasciurus hudsonicus)

Common Names – Spruce squirrel, pine squirrel, boomer, chatterbox.

Description – This small tree squirrel has a bushy reddish brown tail, often with a black band near the end, and a distinct white eye ring. The body color changes seasonally. In winter, the coat is bright reddish and the undersides whitish. In summer, the coat becomes duller and a black line develops between the back and undersides. Red squirrels have ear tufts which are present in winter but absent in summer.

Age and Growth – Adults measure 10 to 15 inches from head to tip of tail and weigh 5 to 9 ounces, making them the smallest of the tree squirrels in their range. Red squirrels live up to 10 years.

Senses – Eyesight, hearing and sense of smell; very good.

Sign – Piles of husked pinecones, or *middens,* are found below red squirrel feeding perches. Some piles contain a bushel or more of husks and mark feeding spots used by generations of squirrels. The nests are slightly smaller than those of gray squirrels and normally built at the junction of a branch and the trunk of a conifer tree. Holes in trees may also indicate a squirrel den. Tracks (p. 123) are seldom seen, except in mud or snow.

Social Interaction – Each red squirrel has its own feeding territory, which it marks with scent secreted from glands in the corners of its mouth. Once the young are large enough to survive on their own, the female chases them away, forcing them to establish their own territory.

Red squirrels are very vocal, often challenging intruders with a lengthy "cherr" or a series of barks and coughs. If other red squirrels invade their territory, they aggressively run them off. When aggravated, they twitch their tail and stamp their hind feet.

Breeding – Prior to breeding, males chase females on the ground and through the trees, much like gray squirrels do. Red squirrels mate twice a year, in late winter and again in midsummer. A litter of 2 to 7 young is delivered about a month later.

Habitat – Red squirrels are found throughout most of Canada and Alaska and many of the northern and Rocky Mountain states. They prefer mature conifer or mixed hardwood-conifer forests.

Food Habits – Red squirrels feed early and late in the day. They tend to be more active at night than most other squirrels. They can tunnel through deep, powdery snow in winter to find food.

Red squirrels eat a variety of seeds, nuts and mushrooms and often chew off whole conifer cones before they ripen, storing them in large caches. They sometimes store an entire winter's food supply in one location.

Movement – A red squirrel's territory is very small, usually an acre or less.

Population – Stable throughout most of the range.

Hunting Strategies – Similar to those used for gray squirrels.

Eating Quality – Very good, although there is not much meat, and old animals can be tough.

Red squirrel in winter coat

Western Gray Squirrel
(Sciurus griseus)

Western gray squirrels look much like eastern grays, but are slightly larger, with darker tails and feet.

Also called *California gray squirrels*, western grays inhabit fairly open pine-oak forests in the Pacific-coast states. They feed mainly on acorns and conifer seeds.

Western grays mate in spring, producing a litter of 3 to 5 young each year. The nests, made of bark and sticks, are built in limbs or crotches of trees at least 20 feet off the ground.

You can hunt western grays the same way you would hunt eastern grays.

Arizona Gray Squirrel
(Sciurus arizonensis)

Although classified as a type of gray squirrel, Arizona grays are more closely related to fox squirrels. Measuring 20 to 25 inches from head to tip of tail, they are intermediate in size between eastern grays and fox squirrels, and the back and shoulders have a rusty tinge. They have a very large, white-fringed tail and white undersides.

Inhabiting only a small region of the southwestern U.S. and Mexico, Arizona grays prefer mixed hardwood forests and usually reside in canyons and valleys. Their food and breeding habits are similar to those of eastern gray squirrels.

Arizona grays can be hunted using the same techniques used for eastern grays.

Douglas' Squirrel

(Tamiasciurus douglasii)

Douglas' squirrels, or *chickarees*, are nearly identical to red squirrels, but their eye ring and undersides have more of an orange tinge. Their mating and feeding habits are also similar, but Douglas' squirrels eat more shoots and berries than reds.

Found in coniferous forests along the Pacific coast, Douglas' squirrels feed mainly on pine nuts. Their populations are cyclical, fluctuating with the annual pine-nut crop. They usually build their large, round nests in conifer trees.

The methods used for hunting Douglas' squirrels are identical to those used for eastern grays.

Abert's Squirrel

(Sciurus aberti)

Also called the *tassel-eared squirrel* because of its prominent ear tufts, the Abert's squirrel is arguably the most beautiful tree squirrel. The body is a dark grizzled gray; the back, reddish; the top of the tail, black and the undersides, white. It is similar in size to the fox squirrel.

Found in parts of Arizona, New Mexico, Utah and Colorado, Abert's squirrels prefer open coniferous forests at high elevations and depend on ponderosa pines for food and nesting sites. Nests are about a foot in diameter and located high in these pines or in juniper trees. They breed in spring, with litter size ranging from 2 to 5.

The Kaibab squirrel, a subspecies of Abert's found along the north rim of the Grand Canyon in Arizona, has a completely white tail and black undersides.

Less wary than other squirrels, Abert's make easy targets because they don't hide behind branches.

Woodchuck

(Marmota monax)

Common Names – Ground hog, American marmot, whistle pig.

Description – A stocky, flat-headed animal, the wood-chuck has a short neck and legs, small ears and a bushy tail. The body is reddish brown to blackish with silver-tipped guard hairs, giving it a grizzled look. The feet are dark brown to black.

Age and Growth – Woodchucks measure 18 to 30 inches from head to tip of tail and weigh 5 to 12 pounds. They live up to 6 years, growing through life. Males are slightly larger than females of the same age.

Senses – Eyesight, excellent; hearing, good; sense of smell, fair. Woodchucks can spot movement several hundred yards away. They scamper into their den if they lose sight of what they were watching.

Sign – Trails through high grass leading to den holes or dirt piles around the holes indicate recent wood-chuck activity. Tracks (p. 123) are seldom seen, except in the exposed dirt around a den hole.

Social Interaction – Woodchucks are solitary, but a pair shares the same den during the breeding season. When alarmed, they make a shrill whistle to warn others of danger. When threatened, they hiss, squeal, growl or grind their teeth. The scent emitted by their anal musk glands enables woodchucks to identify each other.

Breeding – Woodchucks breed in early spring. In their search for a receptive mate, males fight to establish dominance, as evidenced by the scars on the head and shoulders of older males. The litter, delivered in late spring, consists of 2 to 6 young.

Habitat – Woodchucks are found in the eastern U.S. and throughout most of Canada into Alaska. They use a wide variety of habitat, including open woods, forest edges and agricultural areas. Wood-chucks live in dens, which are usually underground burrows up to 30 feet long and 5 feet below ground, with

Typical entrance hole

several entrance holes. They also make dens in rock piles or beneath wood piles and old buildings.

Food Habits – In spring, woodchucks feed mainly in midday; in summer, early and late in the day; in

fall, throughout the day, to build up a winter fat reserve.

Primarily grazers, woodchucks feed on grasses, clover, alfalfa, wild fruits and, sometimes, corn. They occasionally eat insects and small birds.

Movement – Woodchucks are most commonly seen in spring and fall, when they leave their dens to feed during the day. During a summer hot spell, they *estivate,* retiring to their den and dozing off into a semidormant state. In late fall, they dig a new den, usually in a wooded area, where they hibernate through the winter. Their respiration rate and heartbeat slow considerably, and they do not awaken until spring.

Population – Stable and, in some areas, increasing to the point of overpopulation, which results in damage to crop fields, pastures and gardens. Woodchucks benefit from clearing of forests to make farmlands; the edge habitat provides good den sites and food supplies.

Hunting Strategies – Hunters use spotting scopes to locate woodchucks along the edges of fields or woods, usually in the morning. They use varmint rifles, often mounted on tripods, to make accurate, long-range shots.

Trophy Records – No official record; a 30-pounder was taken by a Pennsylvania hunter in 1966.

Eating Quality – Seldom eaten, but young animals have tender meat that tastes much like squirrel. Old animals can be very tough.

Yellow-Bellied Marmot
(Marmota flaviventris)

Common Names –
Rockchuck, yellow-footed
marmot, mountain marmot.

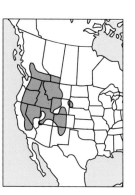

Description – Similar in size
to a woodchuck, it has yellowish to red-orange, rather
than brownish, undersides.
The upper body, feet and tail
are a grizzled yellow-brown.
The head is black, with a
white snout and a white spot
between the eyes.

Age and Growth – Rockchucks measure 20 to 28
inches from head to tip of tail and weigh 5 to 10
pounds. Males usually outweigh females, with
exceptionally large males exceeding 15 pounds.
Rockchucks live as long as 7 years.

Senses – Identical to those of woodchuck.

Sign – A mound of dirt marks the entrance to a den.
The entrance holes, which measure 8 to 9 inches
wide, are usually dug under a boulder that serves as
an observation post. Often, there is a well-worn trail
leading to the den entrance, and some shallow dens
have clumps of dry grass, which is used for bedding
material, visible outside them. The tracks (p. 123)
are rarely seen on the rocky terrain, but resemble
those of woodchucks.

Social Interaction – Highly gregarious, rockchucks
live in colonies and often feed together in large
groups. They whistle to warn others of danger, but
the sound is not as loud as that of a hoary marmot.

Breeding – Males begin searching for a mate as soon
as they emerge from hibernation in early spring. They
may have to tunnel through several feet of snow to
reach the surface. A pair shares a den during the
breeding period, and a litter of 4 to 6 is delivered in
late spring.

Habitat – As their name indicates, rockchucks are
found primarily on rocky terrain, specifically the
rock-strewn slopes, valleys and foothills of mountains
in the western U.S. and Canada. They live at elevations up to 12,000 feet, often establishing colonies
under the buildings of ghost towns left by early min-
ers. They occasionally range into agricultural lands,
particularly where there are alfalfa fields.

Food Habits – Rockchucks feed early and late in the
day, sometimes staying out a little past sunset. If food
is scarce at the high altitude where they live, they
make daily downhill migrations.

They feed on grasses and other green plants; berries,
such as blackberry and service berry and cultivated

crops, especially alfalfa. Where rockchuck populations are high, they can cause serious crop damage.

Movement – Rockchucks spend much of their life underground, hibernating from mid-fall through early spring and estivating during summer hot spells. Despite their stocky build, they effortlessly scamper up and down the rocky slopes.

Population – Stable; because of the rough terrain they inhabit, they are lightly hunted.

Hunting Strategies – Because rockchucks tend to look for danger from below, the best strategy is to climb well above them and take long-range shots with a varmint rifle.

Eating Quality – Seldom eaten, but the meat is very good and has been compared to that of cottontail rabbit. But rockchucks carry the tick that transmits Rocky Mountain spotted fever, so you must be careful when handling and cleaning them.

Hoary Marmot

(Marmota caligata)

Common Name – Whistler.

Description – Largest of the North American marmots, the hoary marmot may grow to twice the size of a woodchuck. The body is a grizzled silver-gray; the rump, reddish brown and the tail, brownish black. The head and shoulders have distinct black and white markings.

Age and Growth – Hoary marmots measure 25 to 30 inches from head to tip of tail and weigh 10 to 20 pounds. They live up to 9 years.

Senses – Identical to those of woodchuck.

Sign – The dens resemble those of yellow-bellied marmots, but the entrance holes are wider, up to 15 inches. Tracks (p. 123) are seldom seen, except in the dirt around the dens.

Social Interaction – Hoary marmots live in loose colonies, but individuals establish and defend their own feeding grounds. They commonly engage in playful wrestling matches.

The loud, shrill call of a hoary marmot explains its common name, "whistler." The call sounds much like a police whistle and warns the colony of impending danger. They also grunt, chatter, growl, and squeal when agitated.

Breeding – The breeding habits are much like those of the yellow-bellied marmot, but the litter usually numbers only 2 to 4.

Habitat – Inhabiting mountainous areas from the northern Rockies into Alaska, hoary marmots are found on rocky slopes and in alpine meadows, often at elevations as high as 8,000 feet.

Food Habits – Hoary marmots feed ravenously during the short summer to build up enough fat to get them through the long winter. They feed throughout the day, heavily grazing the area within 200 yards of their den, and then retire to the den at sunset. Favorite foods include grasses and other green plants, berries and roots.

Movement – Hoary marmots spend their lives in the vicinity of their den, but they may travel several miles when recolonizing or when food becomes scarce. They hibernate from fall to spring, spending only 4 to 5 months above ground.

Population – Stable; because hoary marmots live in such remote locations, they are affected very little by the activities of man.

Hunting Strategies – Climb above them and take long-range shots with a varmint rifle.

Eating Quality – Seldom eaten but very good; similar to cottontail rabbit.

Black-Tailed Prairie Dog
(Cynomys ludovicianus)

Description – The body is reddish to yellowish brown, with a short, black-tipped tail and white undersides. The legs are short and the feet have long, curved claws, used for burrowing.

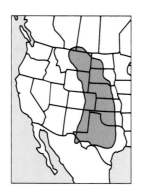

Age and Growth – Blacktails measure 14 to 17 inches from head to tip of tail and weigh 2 to 3 pounds. They live up to 8 years.

Senses – Eyesight, excellent; hearing, very good; sense of smell, fair. They can spot movement at a surprisingly long distance, and they hear warning barks of other prairie dogs hundreds of yards away.

Sign – Volcano-shaped mounds, which measure 1 foot high and more than 2 feet across, mark den entrances. The entrance holes, located at the top of the mound, are spaced 25 to 75 feet apart. Tracks (p. 123) are seldom seen, except around the mounds.

Social Interaction – Black-tailed prairie dogs live in colonies, or *towns,* sometimes consisting of thousands of individuals and covering hundreds of acres. The towns are broken into family groups, or *coteries,* which include 1 to 4 females, the young from the past 2 years and a dominant male, who defends the area against intruders.

Prairie dogs are very vocal, getting their name from their doglike barks and yips. The shrill bark is a warning signal; the yip, an all-clear. They also make several other sounds, including whistles, chirps and squeals. As a gesture of recognition, they "kiss" by cocking their heads and touching incisors.

Breeding – Mating begins in early spring; males breed with all the adult females within their coterie, and each has a litter, averaging 5 young, in late spring.

Habitat – Found on arid, level, shortgrass prairies, mainly in the Great Plains states.

Food Habits – Blacktails feed most of the time they're above ground, which, in spring and fall, is all day. In the heat of summer, they feed in morning and evening; on cold winter days, in midday. They usually graze around their den, seldom venturing more than 150 feet from the entrance.

Primary foods include the leaves, stems and roots of grasses and weeds, but they occasionally eat grasshoppers and other insects.

Movement – When they're not feeding or they detect danger, blacktails retreat to their dens, which are a complex system of tunnels as much as 14 feet deep. The tunnels have several side chambers and may be linked to other dens.

Population – Stable to slightly increasing. By 1980, poisoning by ranchers to eliminate food competition with cattle and prevent cattle from breaking their legs in prairie dog holes had reduced the blacktail population to less than 10 percent of what it was a century ago. Little poisoning is now done, and populations are controlled by hunters and predators. The largest dog towns are found on federal lands.

Hunting Strategies – Hunters scout from a vehicle or talk to ranchers to locate a dog town, and then crawl to within 200 to 400 yards of it. A varmint rifle with a high-power scope is used to locate a target and make a clean kill.

Eating Quality – Fair; the meat has an earthy taste and is seldom eaten.

White-Tailed Prairie Dog

(Cynomys leucurus)

Description – Nearly identical to the black-tailed prairie dog, the whitetail is slightly smaller, with a white-tipped tail and black patches above and below the eyes.

Age and Growth – Whitetails measure 12 to 15 inches from head to tip of tail and weigh 1½ to 2½ pounds. They live up to 5 years.

Senses – Similar to those of the black-tailed prairie dog.

Sign – Dens, which are usually dug on hillsides, lack the volcano-shaped entrance mounds of blacktail dens, and the dirt around them is not packed as hard. Tracks (p. 123) are similar to those of blacktails and found only around dens.

Social Interaction – Whitetails form smaller, looser colonies than blacktails. Their calls are similar.

Breeding – Whitetails mate in mid- to late spring, a few weeks later than blacktails. Males begin searching for a mate soon after they rouse from hibernation, but, unlike blacktail males, they breed with only one female each year. The litter, averaging 5 young, is delivered in early summer.

Habitat – Found primarily in Colorado, Wyoming and Utah at elevations of 5,000 to 10,000 feet, whitetails live on shortgrass and sagebrush plains, sometimes sprinkled with pines and junipers. The underground portions of their dens are much like those of blacktails, but are less likely to be linked to other dens.

Food Habits –Whitetails feed throughout the day in spring and early fall, but only in morning and evening in the heat of summer. They often double their springtime weight by hibernation time.

They eat a wide variety of grasses, woody plants and roots, feeding on saltbush and sagebrush when other foods are scarce.

Movement – White-tailed prairie dogs normally stay within 50 feet of their den, except when the young disperse to establish a new territory. Unlike blacktails, they hibernate up to 6 months of the year, beginning in early fall.

Population – Stable to slightly increasing; poisoning has nearly ended and numbers are rebounding in many areas. Colorado and Wyoming presently have a program to increase white-tailed prairie dog populations, for the purpose of bringing back the endangered black-footed ferret, which depends on them for food.

Hunting Strategies – Identical to those used for black-tailed prairie dogs.

Eating Quality – Similar to the blacktail.

Marsupials
Order Marsupialia

The order *Marsupialia* includes about 250 species found throughout the world, but only one, the opossum, is found in North America. Marsupials differ from most other kinds of mammals in that they do not have a *placenta* linking the fetus to the uterus. The female has a belly pouch, or *marsupium*, which covers the teats and holds the young until they are large enough to take care of themselves. Marsupials have smaller, more primitive brains and more teeth than other mammals.

Opossum
(Didelphis virginiana)

Common Names – Possum, Virginia opossum, common opossum.

Description – Resembling a large rat, the opossum has a round, naked, whitish tail; a white head with thin black ears, usually with white tips; a pink nose and white undersides. In the North, the upper body is grayish white; in the  South, grayish brown to black. About the size of a house cat, the opossum has short legs, and the hind feet have a thumblike first toe, enabling them to grip objects such as tree branches.

Age and Growth – The young are tiny at birth, only the size of a navy bean, and very poorly developed. They grow to full size in 10 months and may live as long as 7 years. Adults measure 24 to 34 inches from head to tip of tail and weigh 4 to 15 pounds.

Senses – Sense of smell, excellent; hearing and night vision, good; eyesight, fair.

Sign – Tracks (p. 123) are often seen along muddy streambanks. The rear print is very distinctive, resembling that of a human hand.

Social Interaction – Solitary animals, opossum are normally secretive and silent, but they hiss, growl or bare their teeth when threatened. When cornered, they sometimes roll over and "play possum" (right), feigning death until the threat disappears.

Breeding – Opossum usually mate twice a year, in midwinter and late summer. In the southern part of the range, they may mate 3 times. Males breed all receptive females they can find, and 5 to 14 blind, naked young are born less than 2 weeks later. To survive, they must crawl up the belly of the female and into her pouch, where they attach themselves to a teat.

Habitat – Found throughout most of the U.S. and Mexico, with the main exceptions being the Rocky Mountain states and the desert Southwest, opossum prefer open deciduous woodlands near agricultural areas and water. They make leaf nests in brush piles, hollow logs and abandoned woodchuck or skunk burrows.

Food Habits – Opossum feed mainly at night, but they do some feeding during the day in winter, particularly in warm weather.

Opossum will eat most any kind of food, including insects, worms, crayfish, small animals, seeds, grasses, clover, fruits and berries. They commonly feed on road-killed animals, and many opossum also fall victim to vehicles.

Movement – Opossum spend most of their life in an area of about 40 acres. But when food is scarce, they cover much more ground, especially when they're fattening up for winter. Although they do not hibernate, they stay in their dens during long periods of bitterly cold weather.

Opossum have a *prehensile* tail, which they wrap around branches for balance when climbing trees. A young opossum can hang by its tail for an extended period, but the tail is not strong enough to support an adult for very long.

Population – Increasing. Native to the eastern U.S. and Mexico, opossum were introduced in California in the 1920s and gradually spread northward into British Columbia. The native eastern population has also slowly extended its range to the north.

Hunting Strategies – Much the same as those used for raccoon; many opossum are taken incidentally by coon hunters.

Eating Quality – Good; the meat is somewhat oily and similar in taste to that of raccoon.

An opossum "playing possum"

117

Tracks

Intersecting brown bear and caribou tracks

To unravel the daily movement patterns of game, a hunter must learn to recognize and interpret many types of animal sign, particularly tracks.

Tracks are easiest to find and identify in damp soil, wet sand or snow. In damp soil, tracks register the fine detail of toes, claws and heels. In snow or sand, some of the detail is lost.

Nevertheless, most hunters, prefer to track on snow, because they can follow the tracks for a long distance and possibly take the animal that made them. Even if it's not possible to track the animal to within shooting distance, you can still learn a great deal about its movement pattern by *back-tracking*. When hunting deer after a fresh snow, for instance, look for fresh tracks in the morning, and then follow them backward to see where the deer fed at night, where it bedded and what type of cover it used when moving from one area to another. Then, use this information to plan your next day's hunting strategy.

You must learn to recognize fresh tracks. They have sharp, distinct edges. On old ones, the edges are rounded by weathering.

Track patterns help identify the type of animal that made them. Hopping animals leave a repeating four-print set, with the side-by-side hind prints ahead of the staggered front prints. Animals that are walking or trotting leave evenly spaced tracks that are staggered and separated from left to right. Often, the rear prints fall within the front ones, or slightly overlap them. But when running, the same animals leave a repeating 4-print set.

The size and shape of tracks from a given animal may vary depending on the speed it is traveling and the type of ground. In dry sand, for instance, the downward force of an animal's foot displaces some of the surrounding sand, making the print slightly larger than the actual foot size. Running animals may slide a bit when they encounter mud or wet sand, which also makes the prints larger than the foot. Dewclaws of hoofed animals (right) may show on soft surfaces, because the feet sink deep into the ground.

The illustrations on the pages that follow will help you identify the tracks of most North American game animals.

Dewclaws

Hoofed Animals

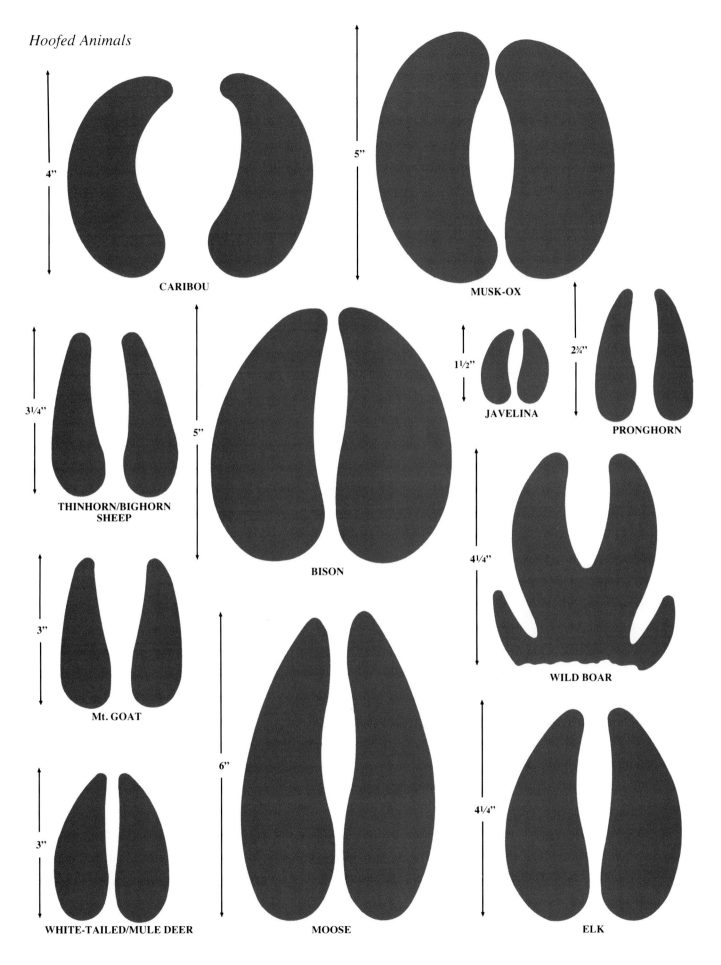

4" CARIBOU

5" MUSK-OX

3¼" THINHORN/BIGHORN SHEEP

5" BISON

1½" JAVELINA

2¾" PRONGHORN

3" Mt. GOAT

4¼" WILD BOAR

3" WHITE-TAILED/MULE DEER

6" MOOSE

4¼" ELK

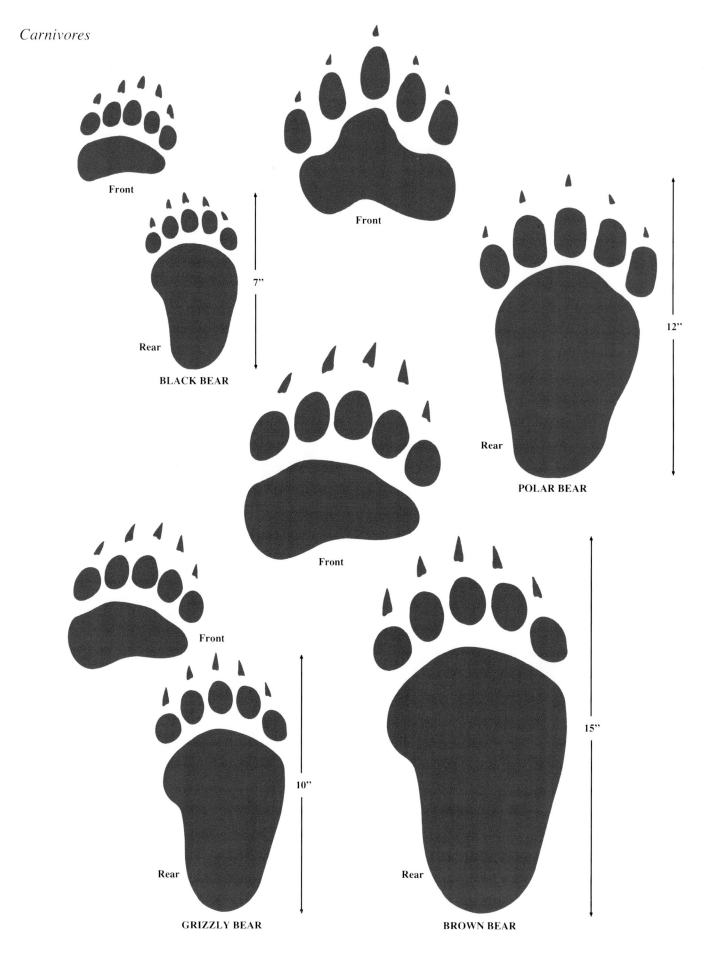

Front

Front

Rear

7"

BLACK BEAR

12"

Rear

POLAR BEAR

Front

Front

10"

Rear

GRIZZLY BEAR

15"

Rear

BROWN BEAR

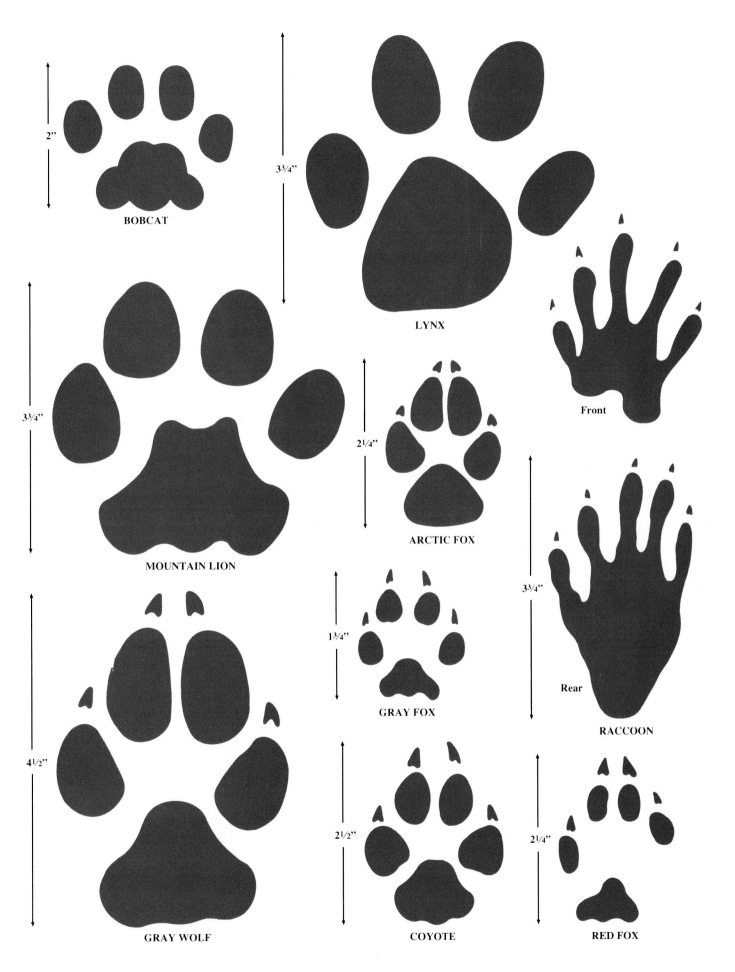

2"

BOBCAT

3¾"

LYNX

Front

3¾"

MOUNTAIN LION

2¼"

ARCTIC FOX

3¾"

Rear

RACCOON

4½"

GRAY WOLF

1¾"

GRAY FOX

2½"

COYOTE

2¼"

RED FOX

121

Rabbits & Hares

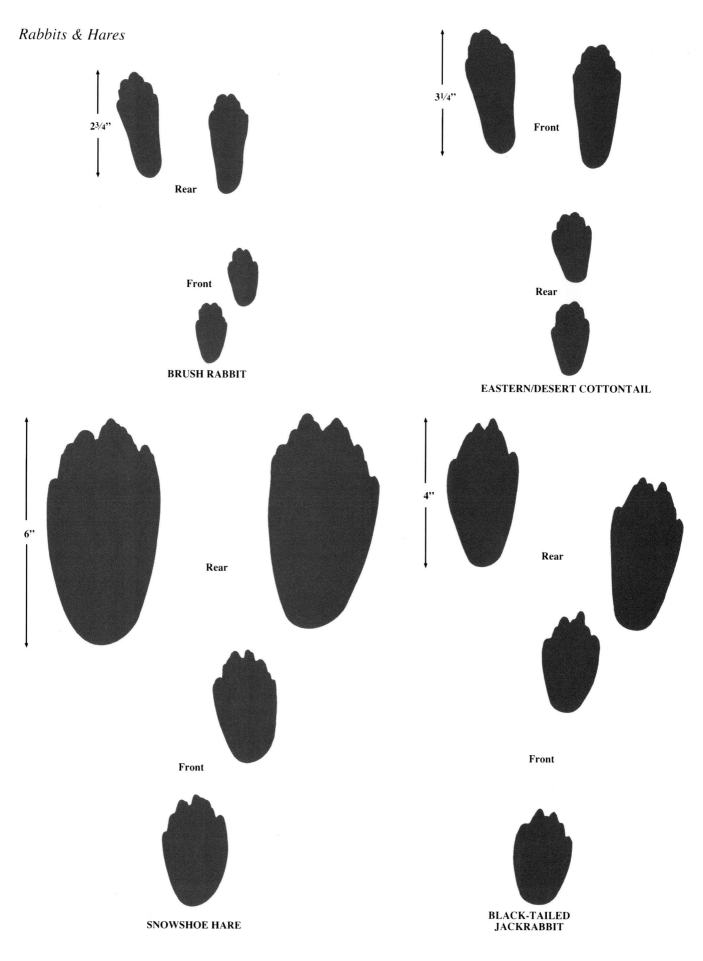

2¾"

Rear

Front

BRUSH RABBIT

3¼"

Front

Rear

EASTERN/DESERT COTTONTAIL

6"

Rear

Front

SNOWSHOE HARE

4"

Rear

Front

**BLACK-TAILED
JACKRABBIT**

Rodents

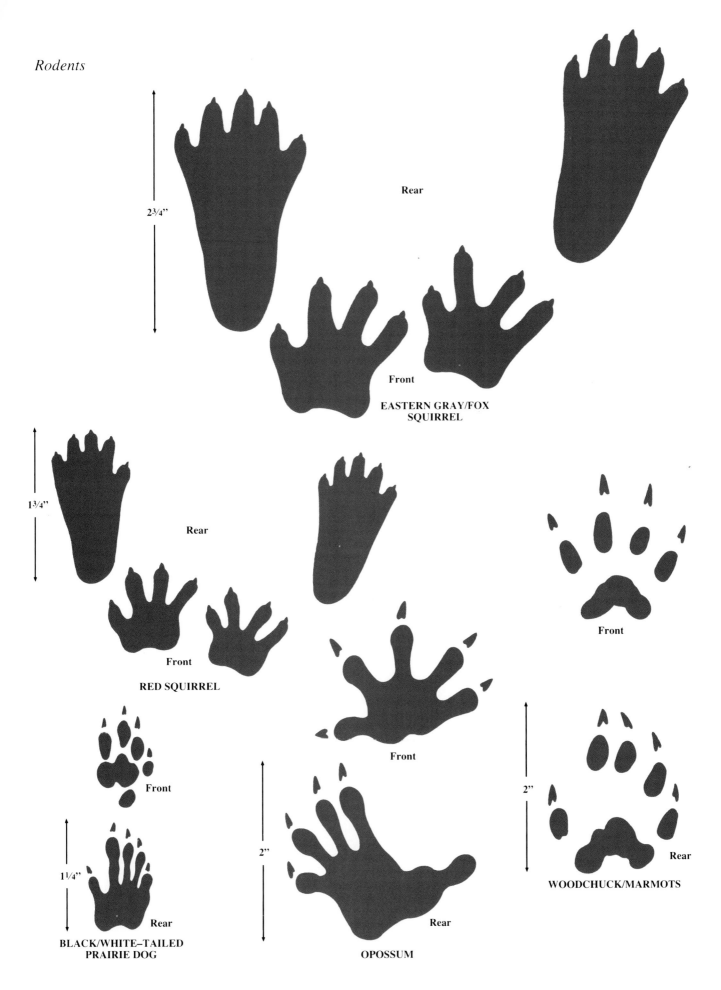

2³/₄"

Rear

Front

EASTERN GRAY/FOX SQUIRREL

1³/₄"

Rear

Front

RED SQUIRREL

Front

Front

Front

Rear

WOODCHUCK/MARMOTS

2"

1¹/₄"

Rear

BLACK/WHITE–TAILED PRAIRIE DOG

2"

Rear

OPOSSUM

2"

Index

Cowles Creative Publishing, Inc.
offers a variety of how-to books.
For information write:
  Cowles Creative Publishing
  Subscriber Books
  5900 Green Oak Drive
  Minnetonka, MN 55343

Contributing Photographers

Note: T=Top, C=Center, B=Bottom,
L=Left, R=Right, I=Inset

Black Sheep Photographics
Lee Kline
2342 Helena Court
Loveland, CO 80537
(970) 667-9919
©Lee Kline p. 94B

Blacklock Nature Photography
P.O. Box 560
Moose Lake, MN 55767
(970) 485-8335
©Craig Blacklock p. 47

The Boone and Crockett Club
Old Milwaukee Depot
250 Station Drive
Missoula, MT 59801
(406) 542-1888
pp. 11L, 11R, 15L, 15R, 27C, 35TR

Denver Bryan
P.O. Box 368
Bozeman, MT 59771
(406) 586-4106
©Denver Bryan pp. 8-9T, 29, 66-67T, 118C

Dembinsky Photo Associates
©Mike Barlow p. 41
©Jim Battles p. 85
©Dominique Braud pp. 10TR, 26TR,
67TR, 100IL
©Sharon Cummings pp. 78-79, 102
©John Gerlach pp. 21BR, 93, 105
©Anthony Mercieca p. 55
©Skip Moody pp. 8C, 100, 103BR
©Alan G. Nelson pp. 64-65
©Ted Nelson p. 22TL
©Stan Osolinski pp. 18BR, 21BL, 37BL
©Dusty Perin p. 115
©Rod Planck pp. 56TR, 86, 94I, 114
©Jim Roetzel pp. 60, 61, 70

Jeanne Drake
8032 Hackberry Drive
Las Vegas, NV 89123
(702) 361-0060
©Jeanne Drake pp. 4, 9B, 26TL, 55I, 56TL,
57B, 58-59T, 62, 71TC, 72-73

Michael H. Francis
2423 Ash Street
Billings, MT 59101
(406) 245-4365
©Michael Francis pp. 14TL, 33, 34-35

The Green Agency
Roper Green
P.O. Box 74
Belgrade, MT 59714
(406) 388-9549
©Bill Buckley p. 96T

Gary Kramer
P.O. Box 903
Willows, CA 95988
(916) 934-3873
©Gary Kramer pp. 12I, 13T, 13I, 37R, 68

Lon E. Lauber
Outdoor Photographer/Writer
2800 Whispering Woods Drive
Wasilla, Alaska 99654
(907) 373-2371
©Lon E. Lauber pp. 13C, 42, 43, 74I

Tom & Pat Leeson
P.O. Box 2498
Vancouver, WA 98660
(360) 256-0436
©Tom & Pat Leeson pp. 38-39

Steve Maas
10641 Smetana Road
Suite 317
Minnetonka, MN 55343
(612) 988-9278
Cover
©Steve Maas pp. 10CL, 10BL, 16, 18T, 20-21,
22-23, 24, 24I, 26BL, 28, 31, 32, 35BL, 36,
37TL, 53, 54, 57T, 71TL, 113, 118BR

Bill Marchel
Outdoor Observations
8322 Saint Mathias Road S.W.
Fort Ripley, MN 56449
(218) 829-3986
©Bill Marchel pp. 71BL, 81

Minden Pictures
24 Seascape Village
Aptos, CA 95003
(408) 685-1911
©Jim Brandenburg pp. 95, 95I
©Michio Hoshino pp. 6-7, 27T, 75

Natural Exposures
16595 Brackett Creek Road
Bozeman, MT 59715
(406) 686-4448
©Daniel J. Cox p. 74T

Photo Researchers
60 East 56th Street
New York, New York 10022
(212) 758-3420
©F. Gohier p. 80
©G.C. Kelley p. 106B
©Tom & Pat Leeson pp. 107T, 107B
©Anthony Mercieca p. 88

Publiphoto
797, av. Champagneur
Outremont, (Montreal) Qc
H2V 3P9 Canada
(514) 273-4322
©D. Levesque p. 26BR

Rocky Mountain Elk Foundation
2291 West Broadway
Missoula, MT 59802
(406) 523-4500
Courtesy of Rocky Mountain Elk
Foundation p. 19

Lynn and Donna Rogers
145 West Conan Street
Ely, MN 55731
(218) 365-4460
©Lynn Rogers pp. 50, 52

Ron Spomer
1830 Highway 99
P.O. Box 760
Troy, Idaho 83871
(208) 835-8383
©Ron Spomer p. 17C

Tom Stack & Associates
977 Elkton Drive
Colorado Springs, CO 80907
(719) 593-1100
©Nancy Adams p. 45BL
©L. Brock p. 44
©Mary Clay pp. 30, 40
©Victoria Hurst p. 90
©G. C. Kelley pp. 12I, 45TR, 97B
©Thomas Kitchin pp. 51R, 100IR, 103BL, 106TR
©Joe & Carol McDonald pp. 116, 117
©Joe McDonald pp. 65TR, 89, 108-109
©Mark Newman pp. 48-49
©Rod Planck pp. 90I, 94
©Milton Rand p. 83
©Leonard Lee Rue III p. 97T
©John Shaw pp. 98-99
©Richard P. Smith p. 51L
©Wendy Stattil/Bob Rozinski pp. 12TL, 14TR
©Greg Vaughn p. 17T
©Robert Winslow p. 69
©AE Zuckerman p. 59B

Texas Inprint
8588 Northwest Plaza Drive
Suite 315
Dallas, Texas 75225
(214) 361-2276
©David J. Sams pp. 18BL, 46, 82

Wild Side of Life
Robert Campbell
6543 E. Placita Elevada
Tucson, AZ 85750
(520) 577-8494
©Robert Campbell pp. 14B, 77, 110-111

Wildstock
Erwin and Peggy Bauer
P.O. Box 987
Livingston, MT 59047
(406) 222-7100
©Erwin and Peggy Bauer p. 71